My Sanctuary

Linda L. Beck

Linda S. Beck

ISBN: 978-0-578-02099-0

ACKNOWLEDGEMENTS

The stories in this book were the true events that happened during my life. They are dedicated to God the Father, the Son, and the Holy Spirit. He guided me through many storms and helped me to write these adventures to share with others.

I wish I had written down every episode when people expressed their appreciation for how my stories, my attitude, and beliefs have inspired them. So many folks have said over the years that I should put this book together; so this is to express my appreciation to everyone that called, or ever stopped to speak with me about my writing. Your compliments were the highlights of many challenging days.

To my old friend, Pat, I owe thanks for proofreading to find my many punctuation errors in the final weeks before publication.

I am especially grateful to my daughter, Sherry, for the hours she spent formatting these stories, correcting my computer errors, and tolerating my changes. In the final hours, she gave me a new nickname – Space Cadet. (It seems I used the space bar on my computer too much and the indent button, not enough.)

And special thanks to her husband Jeff for his computer support and to both of them for the gift of a new computer. (Although, at first, I could have *killed* them.)

To my daughter, Sonya, for the DVD's of several church services that gave me stories to write. And, special thanks, for the gift of grandchildren she has given me. (Stories for another book, maybe?).

I will always be thankful to my fellow writer and friend, Evelyn Allison, for encouraging me to send my first stories for publication in Senior Savvy and The Salisbury Post.

I am a blessed person with so many friends and loved ones, it would be impossible to list all of you; but I will always be grateful to everyone who has shared my life.

EMBARKING ON ANOTHER ADVENTURE IN MY LIFE AS A WRITER

Once when I shared the exciting news that a national magazine had bought one of my stories, my friend asked if I had always been a writer. That's a difficult question to answer unless one knows the definition of "writer." An antiquated dictionary in my possession defines writer as "a person who has written something specified, or a person who writes as an occupation." Well, I don't write to earn a living, but I suppose I have written many specific thoughts.

The next question friends ask is always when, and how, I got started writing. I remember someone gave me a diary as a teenager, and I suppose that is where, and when, I first recorded my thoughts on paper. I still have that "secret" diary tucked away in a closet, but I've lost the key. My trip journals were the first writings that I shared with friends. I was told then that I should be a writer. Some folks would say they felt they were traveling right with us.

English and spelling were my favorite subjects in school, and I fared well there, but I've forgotten a lot of the punctuation and grammar rules. There will be some errors in this book, but I hope folks will remember that I write as I think, and that seldom includes commas. I like exclamation points because they show excitement! There may be a lot of those since there's been some excitement in my life.

I've always loved words. My introduction to the dictionary came when questions were answered with "look it up." That caused me to check the spelling and definition of words, and created within me the desire to learn more. Electronic spell-checks and computers were unknown in those days, and have no place in my heart today. I still do not write my stories on the computer; I write them in my recliner with pen and paper; then type them after I've finished. Sometimes I call it my "prayer chair" because some of these stories require a lot of prayer!

With age, I find myself having to double check the spelling of words I'm sure I once knew.

But even now, it is a challenge to look up strange words or recheck old familiar ones.

I think a writer must first be a reader. I've always loved to read. Most of us can't remember a time when we couldn't read. My adventure in becoming a Laubach tutor caused me to appreciate the English language even more. Helping someone else improve his or her reading skills, reminded me how learning something new can be so challenging. I remember when I used to always study the words and definitions in Reader's Digest. I still find myself turning to that page when I come across the magazine in a doctor's office.

Helping teach my grandsons to read has also renewed my interest in words. Sometimes when we speak to children, we assume they understand what a word means. We can show them objects or identify actions, but it is more of a challenge to define emotions or thoughts.

Education is so important for children. One of the best examples of this is a story I heard, and have told many times. I don't know who the original author was, but any word can be inserted and be proof of what we sometimes expect of children, before we really teach them. The story goes like this:

> A father took his little girl for a walk in the woods. She ran ahead and he warned her to stay on the *path*. She immediately veered off into another direction. He ordered her to stop and come back. He repeated himself, and she asked, "Daddy, what's a *path?*"

Most of my writing consists of basically a thousand or so English words. I tend to use clichés, which are avoided by famous authors. But then again, according to the dictionary, an author should be the "original" writer of a literary work, or one who practices writing as a profession.

Well, except for clichés, my writings are original thoughts even if they are not great literary works. Even though many folks say I should write a book, this assortment of stories is my life, one chapter at a time. All of these stories are true events that happened, but may not be in chronological order.

Maybe I should really be called a "thinker." Let's see, my dictionary defines a thinker as a person who devotes his time to thought or meditation. Yes, I tend to do that a lot; but then there are those times when I just have to write those thoughts down, more frequently lately, lest I forget them. I guess that's why my friends are nice enough to call me a writer.

In the beginning, some of the stories were just journal entries; but after a few were published, I decided it was easier to write my thoughts just once.

Many years ago, I did take a creative writing class and even wrote a few fiction stories. These stories have remained buried in a file cabinet until I recently pulled them out for revision. One has been entered in a contest, and another has been submitted to a magazine. I don't have high hopes for either, as fiction is not my first love, even when I read. But what do I have to lose; there's that old cliché: "Nothing ventured, nothing gained."

This reminds me of my other love - collecting famous quotations. I suppose my "secret" desire is to be the author of famous quotations; but alas, that's not my gift, so I collect and use the famous quotations of others.

After my husband died, I enrolled in a correspondence writer's class, and that encouraged me to develop my personal writing style. It has been my desire for these stories to be conversations with friends. Hopefully all readers will be able to relate to my experiences. I try to emphasize my thoughts by using italics, capitalization, underlining, parentheses, etc. The encouragement of friends, and even strangers, led me to search for places that would consider publication of my stories. Recognition as a writer has been one of the highlights of my life; and the possibility now of selling my stories as a book is another new adventure.

A PRESENT-DAY SAMARITAN

Standing in the lobby of the Grand Hotel at New Heritage USA, I was in awe of the size and grandeur of the place! Since reading about the retreat for disabled families in Charlotte, I had felt a voice guiding me in making the necessary arrangements. In two days everything had fallen into place, but after looking around, I wasn't sure if I should have come.

Although I had traveled with a disabled man and his wife, I was really on my own now. Because of my multiple sclerosis, this put me in a precarious situation. My physical limitations would dictate how involved I could become and I realized that the sheer size of this place would be yet another handicap. I was beginning to worry that coming alone might have been a mistake!

I heard myself being paged and then I met my roommate, Alice. I had been told I would room alone, but for some reason the plans had been changed. I thought I was disabled, but Alice was in a wheelchair and had flown alone from

New York. It quickly became obvious that Alice was struggling to maneuver her wheelchair.

"Alice, would you like for me to push you?"

"Well, dear, that would be so kind, but you seem to have trouble walking. Are you strong enough?"

"I will be glad to help as much as I can, but I have MS so I may have some problems."

"Oh, Linda, I have multiple sclerosis, too." Alice said.

I felt a vise gripping my chest as I realized I could be just like this elderly wheelchair-bound lady someday. I was getting very fatigued and depression weighed heavily on my shoulders!

After helping Alice get settled, I rested for awhile. Then I prayed for strength to freshen my hair and makeup for the dinner meeting.

"Alice, are you ready for dinner?"

"Almost, I can't do anything with my hair because it's hard to keep my arms up long enough."

"Would you like for me to use my curling iron on your hair?"

"Linda, would you really do that? Nobody has ever done anything like that for me except my beautician."

"Well, I'll try if you're brave enough to let me," I laughed. "But I warn you, I've never done it for anyone else either except my mama."

Alice hugged me and I noticed tears in her eyes. I couldn't figure what prompted me to volunteer to do her hair. That was totally out of character for me. I hardly knew this lady, and I wondered why she had come alone since she seemed to need so much help. We continued to chat as I used the curling iron. I was beginning to feel very close to Alice as we talked about our lives. I turned her toward the mirror. "What do you think?" I asked.

"Linda, it looks really nice!" she squealed. "Thank you so much! You have been very helpful. I'm beginning to wonder how I survived three days without you."

"Why have you been here three days? I thought the retreat only started today."

"I had to fly in Saturday to get the reduced rate."

I was astonished that Alice had been here alone for three days. No wonder she was tired. I had only learned about the retreat on Sunday and had been in a mad rush to get in before the deadline. It amazed me that things worked out for me to attend.

"Well, Alice, I'm glad you like your hair," I said. "Let's go eat; I'm famished." It was so far to the dining room that I had to rest three times.

By the time we arrived, I needed Alice's wheelchair because normally I can't walk long distances without my own wheels. I was amazed that I even managed to help Alice get her food. Then we sat down to meet our dinner companions.

We felt honored when Joni Eareckson Tada joined us. Joni helped everyone get acquainted and began to tell us about the JAF Ministries. The excitement of meeting her and the anticipation of what was ahead camouflaged the sheer exhaustion.

Joni asked everyone what had brought us here and when I shared my feelings, she smiled and said she believed God had a purpose in my coming and that it would be revealed. I loved her immediately and I knew this was going to be a rewarding week!

As I began to observe the many disabled children around us and watched Joni coping with her own disabilities, I began to feel that I was one of the fortunate ones!

After the festivities were over, and I had pushed Alice back to our room, I collapsed on my bed too exhausted to even undress. I prayed that the Lord would equip me with enough strength to get through this retreat. I fell asleep as I prayed for God's guidance.

"Help me! Please help me! I need to go to the bathroom and I can't get up!"
Awakened from a deep sleep at 5:00 am, I sat straight up in bed wondering how Alice expected me to help her. I was so totally exhausted from the stress of the previous day that I wasn't sure I could even get out of bed!

I prayed for God to help me and then struggled over to pull Alice to a sitting position. Working together, we got her into the wheelchair and I collapsed back on the bed. I wondered how I would make it three more days.

As I prayed for strength and answers, a picture of the biblical Good Samaritan (Luke 10:25-37) appeared before me. My eyes flew open and I sat straight up. "That must be the answer," I whispered.

I realized that the Lord had led me to be Alice's Good Samaritan and He would guide me! I needed to stop worrying and wait on the Lord. What I needed to do would be reveled to me.

Almost immediately, I realized the biggest problem with the wheelchair was that Alice had forgotten to bring the footrests and had to drag her feet. I snapped to attention, turned to the nightstand, and pulled out the phone book. I would rent her a different wheelchair. After a few phone calls, I found a shop at New Heritage. I told Alice about my plan as we dressed for breakfast.

As we proceeded down the long corridor of specialty shops, another Good Samaritan stepped up and offered to push Alice the rest of the way. I stopped to rest and yet another Good Samaritan showed up with an empty wheelchair for me.

There was no longer a doubt in my mind that God had guided me to this retreat to learn more about sharing and caring for disabled neighbors. Once Alice and I were settled, I became aware that there were Good Samaritans everywhere.

Many teenagers had volunteered and paid their own way to serve as caregivers for the disabled children. This gave the parents a mini-vacation. The children benefited because someone ministered to them as if they were normal kids on vacation.

Some families knew one another from other JAF retreats and soon we all knew each other. The love of Christ was evident everywhere. Finally, I knew why I had been led to New Heritage and there was no longer any question in my mind whose voice had guided me there! The Lord had been my travel agent. He wanted me to see that even disabled people can minister to others and that I could still feel useful in spite of my disability.

I thought about His commandment to love one another (John 13:34). Never before had I felt such love and compassion among strangers. Having followed His will in my life, I had been truly blessed.

Each time I struggled down the main corridor, my eyes were drawn to a huge ornate frame with this verse from Isaiah 40:31...

"But those who hope in the Lord will renew their strength.

They will soar on wings like eagles; they will run and not grow weary, they will walk and not be faint."

(1994)

WHEREVER HE LEADS

Over the years I had written journals, speeches, and stories; but when my husband died in 1993, I lost interest in writing. After his death, I rededicated my life to the Lord and started reading and studying God's word. One day I was praying about my personal prayer life and the fact that I couldn't adequately voice my feelings. I asked the Lord to help me express my feelings better as a witness for Him.

Upon completing my prayer, I picked up my daily scripture book. My eyes nearly popped out as I read another writer's feelings of being like Moses… "slow of speech and slow of tongue." (Exodus 4:10) The writer said that with God's help she was a "prolific writer" and could use her writing skills to witness for the Lord. Well, that got my attention, and I thought about all the people who had often encouraged me to write. I certainly was not a "prolific writer," but perhaps I could improve my skills and with God's help also learn to witness for Him through my own writing.

I began to feel very excited as if the Lord were trying to tell me something.

I called my brother, Mike, and asked him if maybe this was one of those "mountaintop experiences" that we had heard about during our recent revival. He suggested that I write a few inspirational articles just to see how they would sound.

The following Sunday I was reading the newspaper, and for some reason, I turned to the Insight Section which I had not read in over two years. In bold print, there was an article about the Southern Writer's Conference in Birmingham, Alabama. The remainder of that day I felt pulled to review the workshop information. I called my brother again and asked him if maybe I should consider going to the workshop.

Mike said, "Linda, have you bought your plane ticket yet?"

I said, "What?"

"I think God is trying to get your attention. Maybe it is His will for you to go to Alabama!"

"Mike, do you really believe that God is speaking to me? I didn't actually hear His voice like some people say they do. How will I really know if this is what God wants me to do?"

He said, "Well, I believe He is trying to get a message through to you, and it would be a great experience for you to listen."

"But, Mike, do you think I am physically able to travel by myself to Alabama? I won't have anyone to push my wheelchair, and I can't take my electric cart; so I will have to walk with my cane. You know how weak I get because of the multiple sclerosis."

"Linda, I think if you decide you are being led to do this, you can and will! You have overcome a lot of obstacles in your life. Just pray about it and you will make the right decision."

"Michael, do you know how far it is to Alabama? This will cost a lot of money that I hadn't planned to spend, but if the Lord really wants me to go, that would be a lame excuse, wouldn't it?"

"Sis, think about what Jesus said to his disciples about worrying: "Therefore, I tell you, do not worry about your life, what you will eat; or about your body, what you will wear." (Luke

12:22-34) "Maybe you shouldn't worry so much about your financial future."

After our conversation, I prayed for guidance and began to check the details. Within two days I was registered, had hotel accommodations, and plane tickets. I was very excited and began telling everyone about what was happening in my life. I felt inspired to give my testimony at church and when I finished, several people insisted they felt led to donate money for my trip. At first I was reluctant to take their money, but one man said, "I'm not giving it to you. I'm giving it to God for His work." I was in awe of the influence my testimony had on him. I began to realize that God really was at work in my life.

In less than three days, I had talked to more people about God's will than I had my entire life. Everyone was praying for me and encouraging me to go. I felt very blessed as my brother took me to the airport and promised to be there waiting for me when I returned.

At the gate, he said, "Take care of yourself and have a great time."

"Now don't you worry about me," I said as I watched the tears well up in his eyes.

He cupped his hands and said, "I'm not worried about you because you're in God's hands. Now go with God." He hugged me tightly and disappeared into the crowd.

The flight to Alabama was very smooth, and I spent this time praying and thinking about all the things that had happened to me over the years. Having been diagnosed with three major health problems, I had not been able to work since 1979. Then in 1993, my husband of 27 years died with cancer. I sold our home, vehicles, etc., and moved to an apartment at the edge of town. I bought an electric cart to use for short errands, and family and friends provided transportation elsewhere.

My life changed drastically again as it had each time I had become ill. Both my daughters married and I found myself alone for the first time in my life. During my grief, however, I realized the Lord had always been there waiting for me to call on Him. The most important thing I ever did was rededicate my life to the Lord! I became involved in God's work at church and began reading and studying the Bible. Maybe attending this writer's conference would help me learn to share God's word.

I laughed to myself as I recalled a conversation with my friend, Gloria, who had always encouraged me to write about my experiences. I had said, "Gloria, I might be embarking on a new career. Maybe I will be a late bloomer like Grandma Moses."

In her humorous way, she laughed and said, "Well, that's better than dying on the vine." We were joking around, but I realized I felt the most alive I had in a long time. Seriously, however, I knew that following God's will in my life was the most important factor.

When I arrived in Birmingham, I realized this trip was going to be a real physical challenge. I was not prepared for the hilly terrain or the huge campus at Samford University. As I struggled to walk, I regretted not having my electric scooter. During that time in my life, I was not a very outgoing person, but I met friendly people everywhere. My disability was evident and these fellow Christians embraced me and offered to help in many ways. It was my first experience in such a Christian atmosphere, other than at church, and the love of God was evident all around me.

The workshops were interesting and helpful and I was delighted that I had made the trip from North Carolina. Although physically exhausting, the trip was mentally and spiritually uplifting and I felt like a new person!

During the closing ceremony, we were asked to share our feelings about why we had come. I felt the Lord nudging me to my feet, and I began to share the events that had brought me to Alabama to a Christian writer's conference. When I finished speaking, everyone applauded. Afterwards, strangers told me how much I had inspired them. They, too, felt that the Lord had led me there to witness for Him. Several of them encouraged me to write about this experience because they believed it would be one of many inspirational articles I would write. Well, it's finished and if it is indeed the Lord's will, I will write many more. As the verse goes in the song, "Wherever He leads, I will go!"

GOD CALLS
IN MYSTERIOUS WAYS

I have never considered teaching as one of my spiritual gifts and doubted my ability. I did not feel I knew God's Word well enough. I'm not really sure by what yardstick I measured this, maybe one of excuses and self-doubt.

One year when our church was preparing for Bible school, a call for teachers was issued. In the past, my choice position had been taking care of teachers' babies. One day our organist, Maoma Penley, said she wished we would have an adult class in Vacation Bible School. I replied, "Well, make your wishes known."

In her forthright manner she said, "I thought I just did!" I explained to her that I was not the director and that I wasn't sure if we would have enough teachers unless we changed to evening classes. She suggested that I teach an adult class. I told her I didn't believe I was qualified to teach.

Maoma looked me over and said, "You can read a teacher's book, can't you?" Well, I had never thought about it like that. I suggested that she pray about it, and I would think about the possibility. I talked to the director and asked if she could get the literature for me to review before I made the decision.

I went to the first workers' meeting, picked up the adult teacher's book, and just flipped it open at random. As my eyes dropped to the third paragraph, I read:

"When you are plagued with butterflies in your stomach, sweaty palms or nervous knees, remember the words of Moses to the terrified people being pursued by the Egyptian army: 'Do not be afraid. Stand firm and you will see the deliverance the Lord will bring today.' (Exodus 14:13).

Surely, if God was able to make a dry path for His people to pass through the Red Sea, He is able to make a way for you to serve Him through teaching His word."

After reading silently, I shared this paragraph with the director and several others. It was evident to each of us that Maoma's prayer had been answered. God calls us to serve in mysterious ways, and He uses others to get our attention when He desires our service. Being used by God as a prayer warrior, organist, teacher, evangelist, or anything else is a privilege and honor.

Needless to say, I started preparation for a Bible study on Faith. I surveyed to see for how many people I needed to prepare, and only six people made commitments to attend. Since we had not had an adult Bible School during the four years I had attended Enon, I decided to prepare for ten people. Several people cautioned me that was a low number, but I was certain that no others would be interested.

When opening night rolled around, my six committed people showed up, then a few more, and more; I was in total shock when 26 people appeared in the conference room. I think many people were pleasantly surprised. Some even joked, "Oh, ye of little faith." This teacher, who had prepared to teach a study on faith, had not set a very good example of faith in God's plan for this Bible School.

In 2 Timothy 2:15, Paul instructs us to "Do your best to present yourself to God as one approved, a workman who does not need to be ashamed and who correctly handles the word of truth." (NIV)

Maoma is one of God's workmen who needs not be ashamed. She sowed the seed and prayed for the harvest. God used her to give me the initiative to answer His call to teach that class.

THE ANCHOR HOLDS

I'm always spiritually moved by how the
Lord gives people the creative ability to take
scripture and mold the words into songs. Then
someone else uses their God-given talent with
musical instruments to put it all together to form a
song of inspiration, hope, joy, praise, and so on.
Sometimes one person has the privileged talent of
being the song writer, instrumentalist, and
performer. Other times the songs are shared by
singers whom God chooses to bless with one
talent – a beautiful voice.

There are many occasions when these
songs have touched special places in our hearts
and lives. I grew up hearing and loving the old
hymns sung by Southern gospel quartets. Those
hymns had all the above ingredients and music
still touches me in a special way every time I
listen.

The first contemporary Christian song that
really spoke to my heart was "The Anchor Holds"
by Ray Boltz. I didn't hear it sung by him, but by

Jeff Chapman, one of God's singing disciples at Enon Baptist Church.

As the words to this song poured forth from Jeff's heart, my life experiences unfolded in front of me. I knew then that God had put all this talent together, particularly at that time, to show me He was the anchor that had held me steady.

My life had been turned upside down and I felt battered and torn like the sails of a ship on a stormy sea. At that time, my health was failing, my husband had passed away, and I had disposed of most of my worldly possessions. The dreams I had held in my hand had slipped away just as the song says, "like they were only grains of sand." For two years, my life had been like a long dark journey, and at that time I was still uncertain if there would ever be another smooth voyage.

Somehow when Jeff finished singing, I knew God had affirmed his love to me, and I recognized Him as the anchor that would steady my life from thence- forward. Jeff was the instrument God used to teach me that lesson; he and this song will always have a special place in my heart.

I rushed out the following day and purchased a cassette. I played the song over and over and shed buckets of tears as I felt God's presence during my loneliness. My stormy seas did not become calm immediately, and there are still times when another storm blows along; but now I know that God is my anchor and holds me steady during the storms of my life.

Music often opens the heart to the worship experience. When the Holy Spirit is present in the hearts of the singers, they often convey this to the congregation. God then speaks to listeners through the sermon itself. I know, for instance, that I don't remember what the sermon was about that day, but I will never forget the Holy Spirit's presence through the song and singer.

Most Christian singers have the desire to spread the gospel message through song and to praise and worship the Lord with the talent He has bestowed on them. It is sometimes believed that they just enjoy performing before an audience;

sometimes that may be the truth, but it isn't necessarily true if God has called one to sing.

God didn't choose to give me the talent to sing, but He has enabled me to share my experiences with others through speaking and writing my thoughts. I'm sure there are some readers who don't share my feelings, but perhaps the Lord chooses to speak to them differently. Maybe another time, He will speak to their hearts through song.

If you have never heard "The Anchor Holds" by Ray Boltz, perhaps the words here will speak to your heart as they have mine:

I have journeyed through the long, dark night
Out on the open sea by faith alone, sight unknown
And yet His eyes were watching me.

CHORUS
The anchor holds, though the ship is battered,
The anchor holds, though the sails are torn.
I have fallen on my knees as I faced the raging seas,
The anchor holds in spite of the storm.

I've had visions, I've had dreams –
I've even held them in my hand.
But I never knew they would slip right through
like they were only grains of sand.

CHORUS

I have been young, but I am older now
And there has been beauty these eyes have seen
But it was in the night through the storms of my
life
Oh, that's where God proved His love to me.

CHORUS

DO YOU BELIEVE
IN MIRACLES?

Do you believe in miracles? Have you ever felt one taking place in your life? As Christians, we can identify with the miracles which were performed by our Lord and Savior Jesus Christ during the time that He walked on this earth. He made the blind man able to see, raised Jarius's daughter and Lazarus from the dead, and did so many more acts of healing.

During my lifetime (60 years), I've experienced several healing miracles. Some folks tend to look at the negatives instead of the positives and often ask that question, "Why?" Well, I don't know why I've had myasthenia gravis, multiple sclerosis, an AVM (arterio venus malformation) in my brain, and a series of other health problems. But I do know that according to His Holy Word (the Bible); God does not give us more than we can bear. (His plans for me must have been that I would be able to carry a heavy load.) But there have been times when I thought I couldn't deal with another negative happening in my life, and it would be like writing a book to share it all; but I just want to encourage others about the answers to prayer – real modern-day miracles in my life.

There was the period during 1973-1976 when I first experienced the effects of myasthenia gravis. I was finally diagnosed with this rare progressive muscular weakness disease which had the potential of becoming very disabling. I became familiar with several people who had this disease and have since gone to be with the Lord; but after several years of ups and downs, it seems my case is now in remission. (Miracle #1)

In 1976 there was the night I nearly died on the operating table. I can remember hearing someone saying, "We're losing her." I also remember my prayers had been that God would heal the staph infection and enable me to return home to finish raising my two daughters. The healing was a long slow process fraught with many difficulties; but my daughters are now grown and married, and those prayers were answered. (Miracle #2)

Then in November 1990, I was given a double dose of bad news when I was told I have multiple sclerosis, a central nervous system disorder, and an AVM (arterio venus malformation) in my brain. The AVM was identified as the cause of the seizures I had experienced in 1989. A miraculous little pill (dilantin) has controlled the seizure activity since then. Praise God for doctors and medicines! (Miracle #3)

Then there were the four major multiple sclerosis exacerbations in 1992 and the diagnosis of my husband's cancer followed by his death in February 1993. During that extended period of traumatic events, not even the doctors thought I would undergo the healing that led me to driving a car again (after six years of not driving), and being able to walk again, live alone, and learn to swim at age 47. No one realized that God was preparing me to be able to travel and speak for Christian Women's Club, so I could tell other women about our Lord and Savior Jesus Christ. (Me, speak in public?) – Miracle #4)

Then in July 2002, I underwent the worst multiple sclerosis attack I have ever experienced. Everything from my breast down was affected, and I was told I would never walk again. For 29 days, my toes would not even wiggle, and I had to use a transfer board to move from one place to another. Five months later, I was finally able to stand up for the first time after that flare-up. I started using a walker but fell several times, so I resigned myself to using a power chair and an electric scooter which a stranger donated to me. (Miracle #5)

Two years later I was finally able to get in the water at the new YMCA by using the electric lift. To the amazement of everyone, I was able to float and swim again; and with the help of the staff there, I have come so far. And that brings us up to the present. Amazing, God's amazing grace! That's what has been taking place. (Miracle #6)

This summer the Lord has enabled me to "play in the dirt" in the yard at the house he led me to build in 2002. I have been getting stronger and felt the best I have since 2002. The buzzing, tingling feelings in my feet (neuropathy) are calmer, and my legs are doing things they have not been able to do for years. Now, I don't know if God is using that castor oil I read about, but a lot of folks have written the doctor in the newspaper to tell him what great results they get from massaging with this very old medicine; so I've been using it on some painful areas in my body.

Personally, I think I am undergoing another miracle (#7). I'm excited and anxious to see how far God plans to take me this time. It's up to me to be willing and able to follow the path that he provides. His path may be the "one less traveled" as in the quotation that is on a sign I put in my yard: "Take the road less traveled."

EXPECT A MIRACLE

If someone or something told you to "Expect a Miracle," what would you think or do? Could you hear God's voice speaking to you through a person, place, or thing? Meditate on that for a moment; then hold the thought, and read on.

On July 5th, 2002, I suffered a major exacerbation of multiple sclerosis and went down on the concrete in the hospital parking lot. The following day, I was told I would never walk again. Nothing was working below my breast.

My family and close friends were devastated, but those who knew me best refused to believe that diagnosis. They thought I would overcome it, just as I had rebounded from other exacerbations

Personally, I knew this was the most severe one I had suffered. I was having spasms and pain like never before, and other body functions were affected. The road ahead was unfamiliar, and I took a "wait and see" attitude.

I accepted the diagnosis because I didn't have time to cry or complain. I had to work on building upper body strength and transferring myself to and from the bed, shower, vehicle, etc. (James 1:2-4 describes this as follows: "Consider it pure joy, my brothers, whenever you face trials of many kinds, because you know that the testing of your faith develops perseverance. Perseverance must finish its work so that you may be mature and complete, not lacking anything.")

When my body was unresponsive or wracked with pain, I would cry out to the Lord for strength to make the necessary moves. (Philippians 4:13 says: "I can do everything through him who gives me strength.") And then, I would transfer. Later transfers became very hard on my wrists and hands, and the doctor ordered wrist supports which made a major difference in my ability to push myself up. (Another one of those things God used. Hold the thought; then read on.)

I had four weeks of intensive therapy and training, so I could learn to be a fully-functioning paraplegic. Rehab enabled me to return to my new home where I could once again live alone. There were many objections to this, but with the loving help of family and friends, I went home on August 6, 2002.

Another four weeks of trying to maneuver a manual wheelchair on carpet was physically exhausting, and even more emotionally debilitating than the original diagnosis. The road ahead was looking long and frightening, and this vehicle (my mind and body) was beginning to need a major overhaul. There was no point in being angry, though, as anger is not a healing balm. (Ephesians 4:26: "In your anger do not sin. Do not let the sun go down while you are still angry, and do not give the devil a foothold.")

Finally, I received a power chair, and it was a gift from God! He saw my need just as He did in 1993 when He provided me with an electric three-wheel scooter. My optimism returned, and I knew that with God's help, I would regain my patience and perseverance which according to His Holy Word would certainly improve my character. (Romans 5:3-4: "Not only so, but we also rejoice in our sufferings, because we know that suffering produces perseverance; perseverance, character; and character, hope.") It, my character, had begun to need a major overhaul anyway. Reviewing the scriptures daily enabled me to accept the situation, but also to work to improve it.

Other health problems kept taking place, but I was home where I was warm, well-fed by others, and fairly content, except for the emotional pain and physical drain my condition was causing my loved ones. Accepting help from others humbled me, and also shamed me, that I had not done more of that before. God has used this to teach me some lessons I needed to learn.

People were praying for me and asking others in several counties to pray also. God heard and answered these prayers. He used a Christian friend and a stick pin to speak to me on December 19, 2002.

In August after I came home from the hospital, I realized I had lost the stick pin that read "Expect a Miracle." I expressed my regrets to my friend, Priscilla, when she called to see how I was doing. She said it was no big deal, and she would try to find me another one.

With so much going on, I thought little more about it. After all, how important could that little pin be other than as a very thoughtful gift of encouragement from another victim of multiple sclerosis.

By December, I was beginning to be able to stand at a walker when someone helped me get up. Still, I could not raise my feet off the floor, and my knees would buckle after a brief moment or so.

As I was exercising on December 18, my right leg, and then the left, had major spasms, and my feet lifted high off the floor in that same order. I was amazed and decided if a spasm could do that, then maybe I could lift them myself. And I did! Wow, what a surprise! It was even more exciting than when my toes voluntarily started wiggling on the 29th day of my hospital stay when nothing else was working.

I already had physical therapy that morning; and while exercising on the bed, my therapist had commented that my legs were moving easier. And after having felt bad for several days, I knew things were the best they had been for awhile.

Later that day as I sat writing a story, I realized my wrists guards might help me get myself up to a standing position at my dining room table. With one hand on the table and one on the power chair, I pushed up and hunched sideways at the table. I was so excited! (Up! Plop down. Up again! Plop down, ouch bottom hurt! Up, push, try hard, etc.) Somehow, I sensed things changing, and the road ahead began to look brighter with each effort.

December 19th was my daughter Sonya's tenth wedding anniversary, so I invited her to breakfast (one meal I still can cook fairly easily.) After we finished eating, I started to demonstrate what I had accomplished the night before.

Sonya said, "Mama, that's wonderful!" Before we knew what was happening, I had both hands on the table and was standing erect. She and I squealed in delight.

The joy of being off my bottom, for even a moment, is always such a blessing. When I stood erect, I felt like a giant. Later, I was able to stand at the kitchen sink where I could finally see the deep bottom. (Wow, did it need a good scrubbing!)

My therapist was not scheduled to come again until the following day, but I called and beseeched him to come see my progress. He said he would be at my home at 2:00 pm.

After Sonya left for work, I searched my Bible for a verse of scripture that I hoped to use in a children's sermon. I could not find it, but part of another verse caught my eye. It said, "You do not have, because you do not ask God. When you ask, you do not receive, because you ask with wrong motives." (James 4:2&3)

I puzzled over that a bit and felt led to pray as in Philippians 4:4-7: "Rejoice in the Lord always. I will say it again: Rejoice! Let your gentleness be evident to all. The Lord is near. Do not be anxious about anything, but in everything, by prayer and petition, with thanksgiving, present your request to God. And the peace of God, which transcends all understanding, will guard your hearts and minds in Christ Jesus." After months of praying for God's will to be done, on

December 19, I told Him He already knew my heart's desire was to walk again. I also expressed that even a "complete healing" would be welcome if that were not asking with the wrong motive. (James 5:15-16 is given as The Prayer of Faith and reads like this: "And the prayer offered in faith will make the sick person well; the Lord will raise him up. If he has sinned, he will be forgiven. Therefore confess your sins to each other and pray for each other so that you may be healed. The prayer of a righteous man is powerful and effective.")

He knows that one thing I have missed is being able to travel to speak to others about His love for all of us, and to present the Plan of Salvation from our sins. (Romans 3:23; John 10:10, Romans 5:8; Ephesians 2:8-9, Romans 10:9; Romans 6:23)

I love to share with others the many times God has changed my life. But if I can't travel, I can praise Him through writing stories or speaking to local groups.

When my mail came at 1:00 there was a Christmas card from my friend, Priscilla, and another stick pin that read, "Expect a Miracle." Philippians 3:13-14 expresses the feelings I experienced: "Brothers, I do not consider myself yet to have taken hold of it. But one thing I do: Forgetting what is behind and straining toward what is ahead, I press on toward the goal to win the prize for which God has called me heavenward in Christ Jesus."

Another friend, Evelyn, who always has just the right thing to share, sent me a card which read: "The task ahead of you is never as great as the power behind you," and she is so right this time, too.

Romans 8:28 reads, "And we know that in all things God works for the good of those who love Him, who have been called according to His purpose."

To God be the glory for my personal Christmas miracle in the year of the Lord, 2002!

A CRACKED POT
IN GOD'S HANDS

I am a cracked pot! Notice, I didn't say a "crack pot," although there may be some who think I am that, too. And no, I'm not referring to addictions to drugs, like crack or pot. The thing is, I'm a flawed vessel. All of us are, but some people don't like to admit it.

Scripture tells us God is the potter and we are the clay. Clay pots tend to have flaws and often they crack. Sometimes I think I'm like a cracked pot.

This especially came to mind recently when I read a beautiful story about how a cracked pot and a perfect pot, both filled with water, were carried daily along a path from the river. The cracked pot felt it was inadequate to do the job right, because it was seldom full when it arrived back at the master's house. However, flowers flourished along the side of the path on which the cracked pot was always carried. The bearer of the pots assured the pot that it was worthy, as the resulting flowers were fulfilling the master's need as they were watered.

Too often, disabled people feel unworthy. We have physical limitations that interfere with normal life. The reality is, however, that God uses cracked pots and flawed people, if they allow Him to do so.

I once knew a preacher who had Lou Gehrig's disease and was bedridden for many years. His wife said that he felt God's purpose for him was intercessory prayer, and he used that time faithfully to pray for others.

Some people in his condition would have had a difficult time understanding how they could be used for God's glory; and many would have been bitter towards God rather than choosing to honor Him. The spiritual reality is that this man was a real work of art molded and shaped by God's design. There are others like Joni Eareckson Tada who serves God worldwide from a wheelchair. Right here in Salisbury, a handicapped man runs Earthen Vessels Ministry to assist other disabled people.

Having been bedridden numerous times, I can't even begin to compare to these people as a vessel used by God. And yet, I'm discovering more every day how God has used my disability in many ways. Some folks say I should "hang out my shingle," as a counselor to other cracked pots. God has given me an ability to empathize with others who need a listening ear. Often He gives me insight to help others resolve problems. He is widening the doors of opportunity for me to speak about him at Christian Women's Clubs across the state and is challenging me to do so in spite of my health problems.

Can I, or am I willing, to be a flawed vessel in God's plan? I am reminded of the words from a song: "Have thine own way, Lord; have thine own way. Thou art the potter, I am the clay. Mold me and make me after thy will, while I am waiting, yielded and still."

A TOUGH NUT TO CRACK

Some time ago, I started to write a story about walnuts. My brother had picked up a 3-gallon bucket full out back by the fence. He was afraid my scooter might turn over if I ran across one by accident. I couldn't find anyone who wanted to crack them, so I started a story hoping someone would enjoy getting some free walnuts.

Then I got sidetracked with two more important stories and the holidays, so I never finished that story. After awhile, I began to notice shells on my porch, ramp, and driveway. The walnut supply seemed to be dwindling, and I happened to notice a squirrel eating one on my porch.

I first thought about bringing the nuts inside, but decided if I were generous enough to allow the squirrels to eat them, they might stay away from my birdfeeder. Within two weeks, the walnuts were all gone. Could only one little squirrel have devoured all those nuts in that short amount of time? I guess this is the reason I never realized I had a walnut tree, as they must have been "good to the last nut."

This story started as a "piece of fluff" about squirrels and walnuts, but God reminded me I'm a little of both and it went from there. Some folks might say that I am a "hard nut to crack." Just like walnuts, I do have a hard outer shell that has developed over time and shielded me, just as the "armor of God" (Ephesians 6:10-18) shields Christians from the Evil One.

I'm told the inner shell of a walnut is also difficult to crack. As I glanced through the scripture hoping to find a good correlation, I came across Second Corinthians 4:16-18: "Therefore we do not lose heart. Though outwardly we are wasting away, yet inwardly we are being renewed day by day. For our light and momentary troubles are achieving for us an eternal glory that far out weighs them all. So we fix our eyes not on what is seen, but on what is unseen. For what is seen is temporary, but what is unseen is eternal."

At times the outer shell of my body has seemed to be "wasting away" as I suffered the effects of multiple sclerosis. Though the inner shell has suffered also, it has "not lost heart." The "meat" of the walnut is like my inner being, my soul, my relationship with our Lord and Savior, Jesus Christ. That meat is "being renewed day by day" through prayer, the reading of scripture, and listening to God's Word preached by those far more knowledgeable than I am. Mainly, the best part of this hard nut (me) has been learning to see God at work in my life, as he laid out his plans for me.

Like a squirrel, I have at times scampered here and fro, strayed from the path he has laid out, and erred in my ways, but God is always there like the beacon in the song, "The Lighthouse." He has guided me through many long lonely winter days, and I am reminded to "Be at rest once more, O my soul, for the Lord has been good to you (me)." (Psalm 116:7) In the absence of space, I encourage you to read all of Psalm 116.

As I was searching through the scriptures while writing this story, I came across a note I had written in my Bible after the loss of several loved ones and numerous multiple sclerosis exacerbations: "This psalm is a good example of how I felt in 1976, 1990, 1992-93, and 2002." I praise the Lord for being the "light" during those dark times.

Praise our Father God for the "unseen which is eternal."

I CAN DO ALL THINGS

One of my favorite scriptures is Philippians 4:13 where the Apostle Paul says "I can do everything through Him who gives me strength." It is better, however, to go back to Philippians 4:11-13: "I am not saying this because I am in need, for I have learned to be content whatever the circumstances. I know what it is to be in need, and I know what it is to have plenty. I have learned the secret of being content in any and every situation, whether well fed or hungry, whether living in plenty or in want. I can do everything through Him who gives me strength."

I've thought a lot about the word "everything." This scripture does not say that I can only do some things, or a few things, or one thing now and then. It doesn't say that I might be able to do this, or that, or that I possibly can do something else. It doesn't say that I can do something, or anything, once in awhile. It says, "I can do *everything* through Him who gives me strength."

In this verse, it doesn't say that I can do anything on my own or by myself under my own power; it says "through Him (Jesus Christ) who gives me strength." Some folks think I am a strong person, and it does appear on the surface that I am; but any strength I possess is given to me by my Lord and Savior. I love to use this scripture in my personal testimony when I speak to groups.

Due to the limitations of my health problems (myasthenia gravis and multiple sclerosis), some skeptics tend to think there is some question concerning the word *everything*. For example, there is the question: "Well, if you can do everything through Him who gives you strength, why can't you walk?"

The reality here is that God is the one who determines when and how much strength He will give me. (And, He has given me different degrees of strength where walking is concerned.) Over the years I have had decreases and increases in physical strength. The important thing here is, have I had decreases and increases in faith?

When we quote scripture like Philippians 4:13 as being applicable in our lives, we best be sure that we have faith that God can give us the ability to do all things that He calls us to do. Do I have faith that He can enable me to walk again? Of course I do! He already has to some degree. But some folks might wonder why I haven't been totally enabled to walk, or completely healed. Those who have to help me walk out of the pool at the YMCA, or lift me out of the hot tub, may wonder why I can walk in alone, but not out. Others, who have to lift me up out of the floor at home, know that they are the strength that God provides at that time.

I know the Lord has used these times to humble me, and to give me reason to call on Him, and to accept the help of others. I know that He has used these circumstances to give me stories to write, and things to talk about. Yes, I do believe that I can do everything through Him who gives me strength! If it is His will, I will walk again; to what degree will be His decision, but He has given me the opportunity to work towards that goal through therapy and determination. He has provided doctors who care about helping me find solutions to the pain associated with walking.

Physical therapy always helps to some degree. I already walk better than I did after July 4, 2002, when this major multiple sclerosis exacerbation took place. At that time, there were statements made to the effect that I would never walk, swim, float, or drive again. Five months later when I stood for the first time, I told folks that some people just don't know the same God I know! In the years since then, I have done some of all those things through Jesus Christ. To our God and Father be glory forever and ever. Amen!

ARE YOUR BURDENS HEAVY?

Have you ever heard the expression, "God has given me a burden on my heart for this?...that?...him?...her?...etc.?" Have you, yourself, experienced that and shared the occasion with others?

What is a God-given burden? These burdens are a message from God and are generally identified as a heaviness of the heart, spirit, or soul that weighs us down physically, emotionally, mentally, or spiritually. How can we learn to deal with these burdens? All of my Christian life, I've heard it said that God doesn't give us more (burdens) than we can bear.

Well, I certainly seem to have had a lot of burdens to bear during my life. Did I, or do I even now, question "why me?" (It's okay to question God as long as we "listen" for His answers.) Certainly, there have been times when I wallowed in self-pity, but I spent a lot of time reading the Bible and searching for ways to overcome my burdens.

One thing I learned is that God often used this burden (my health) to accomplish His purpose in my life. But health issues have not been my only burdens. Loss of so many of my loved ones has been a heavy burden; and tender-heartedness for the needs of others has, at times, been a burden which caused me a lot of tears.

Dr. Charles Stanley says, "It's important to understand that not all burdens are bad...many of them are very good for us because they direct us to God's purpose for creating us."

The weight of our burdens can seem to bend us over. As our troubles get worse, we tend to slump more and more from the heaviness. Have you ever felt like you had "the weight of the world" on your shoulders? When our troubles get worse, we often sink further into depression, defeat, and despair.

In Luke 13: 10-13, we are told that there was a woman who had been bent over for eighteen years. She was so bent over that she walked looking almost directly at the ground. We don't know exactly from what her problem stemmed, but we know some diseases today which can cause problems like this. The elderly lady in the Bible believed that Jesus could heal her; and even though it was on the Sabbath, she sought him out and he freed her from this burden.

In Matthew 11:28-30, Jesus tells us to: "Come to me, all you who are weary and burdened, and I will give you rest. Take my yolk upon you and learn from me, for I am gentle and humble in heart, and you will find rest for your souls. For my yolk is easy and my burden is light."

When your burdens get heavy, do you call on the Lord and trust Him to answer your prayers? His answer may not be exactly the healing we want it to be; it may not take place where, when, or how we desire, and may be more of an emotional or spiritual healing rather than the physical one for which we asked.

Returning to the issues of my own health, I still have the five neurological conditions; but my real healing took place in my heart and soul when I realized I am a child of the King, our most High God. Through prayer and studying the Bible, I have come to realize that God's purpose has been

to use my illnesses and my losses to help me
"straighten up." (Now if I would just work on
improving my posture, maybe I wouldn't be so
bent over physically.)

I've come so far, and I know He can take
me even further if I do cast my burdens on Him.
In Hebrews 7:25, we are told "Therefore He is
ABLE also to save forever those who draw near to
God through Him, since He always lives to make
intercession for them."

Have you discerned God's purpose in your
creation? Were you called to preach, to teach, to
write, or to share the gospel through mission
work? Have you figured out how to use your
burdens for the benefit of others who need to
know about our Lord and Savior Jesus Christ?

God can lift us up and help us straighten
out those things that have caused us to be so bent
over. Some examples of these are: pornography,
poor marriages, interpersonal relationships,
gambling, anger, and other hindrances in our lives.
He can give us forgiveness, healing, and holiness
if we cast those burdens on Him. Eternal salvation

is a quality of life we experience in the here and now, as well as in the hereafter.

In the garden of Gethsemane, Jesus prayed: "If it is possible let this cup pass from me...yet not as I will but as you will." This "cup of suffering" was permitted as part of God's plan just as sometimes our sufferings are God's purpose in our own generation. But never forget that our God is ABLE to do all things that are His will and plan for each of our lives.

MY GOD IS BIGGER
THAN MY PROBLEMS

God is an awesome God and has the power to help me change my perspective when my load gets too heavy. After listening to a sermon by Joel Osteen, I wanted to share my thoughts with others.

Many of us have afflictions that allow our vision of the greatness of God to be blurred. We sometimes can't see the light at the end of our affliction, because we are unable to rise above our circumstances.

In God's Holy Word, the apostle Paul tells us God will give us the strength to go "through" our problems. In Psalm 23, David said he would walk "through" the valley of the shadow of death. He did not say "over," "under," or "around."

According to the dictionary, an "affliction" is a "condition" of pain, suffering, or distress, or the "cause" of the pain, suffering, or distress. When one is in horrendous physical pain, it can be very difficult to view one's affliction as "light and momentary troubles achieving for us an eternal glory that far out weighs them all." (2 Corinthians 4:17) Second Corinthians 4:18 reads: "So we fix our eyes not on what is seen but on what is unseen. For what is seen is temporary, but what is unseen is eternal."

But if we can compare our afflictions to the greatness of God, it may help us to change our perspective about our problems...physical, spiritual, or emotional. Sometimes this enables one to magnify God, rather than one's affliction.

Perhaps then the decision is that the "affliction" is not in control. Personally, I believe that "...in all things God works for the good of those who love him, who have been called according to his purpose." (Romans 8:28)

It has been my goal that my health problems will not "take away my joy" or the "...peace of God, which transcends all understanding..." (Philippians 4:7) This does not mean that I have not, will not, or do not suffer. To me, it only means that if I stay in faith and believe that God is at work in my life, He can raise me up just as the song, "You Raise Me Up" indicates.

It is good to rise in the morning thanking God for our troubles, as well as our blessings, in spite of our pain and suffering. It is important for us to believe that "God holds us in the palm of His hand and can count the number of hairs on our head."

Osteen closed with a summary of my favorite personal beliefs that are as follows:

"...this, too, shall pass"

"Our Father is a God of restoration"

"Don't look at the size of the problem; look at the size of our God."

"This is the day that the Lord has made, let us rejoice and be glad in it."

"We are responsible for our own happiness. Don't let others steal our joy."

"Be happy where you are, and God will take you where you want to be."

"Train yourself to stay in peace."

If we follow these guidelines, we can be VICTORS instead of VICTIMS just as Joel Osteen claims.

THORNS, THISTLES, & WEEDS

As I rode through my yard pulling weeds, I remembered a story I've intended to write for a long time. Some weeds have thorns, and I caught my finger on one of those. Ouch! There are so many beautiful flowers, but many flowers have thorns. There is an old verse that goes like this: "I can complain because rose bushes have thorns, or rejoice because thorn bushes have roses." (I choose the last because of my love for roses. My life has been rather "thorny," but I'd rather not complain because I know I am a sinner saved by grace.)

When I was just a young bride, my father-in-law (Pop) taught me to use a hoe. In the process of learning how to hoe weeds, unfortunately, I often took the plant with the weed. Sometimes I would cover it up, and hope he wouldn't notice the missing plant. (Is that what we try to do with our sins?) Well, shame on me; but remember, I was a new member of the family then!

Pop was a kind man, and I guess a patient one, because he came to appreciate my *help*! I got better as time went by and eventually taught my two daughters to hoe. (*Boy, did they hate hoeing.*)

I actually got to the point where I enjoyed hoeing, except in the hard red clay. I think some of the pain in my shoulders and hands is a result of pounding a dull hoe in that stubborn dirt all those years. (I guess I should have learned to sharpen the hoe.)

Recently, I met a new friend who commented that while hoeing in their garden, she told her daughter she just didn't understand why God gave us so many weeds and thistles. Madison said she knew where to find that answer, and I told them I had been intending to write this story for years.

After God planted the beautiful Garden of Eden, he warned Adam in Genesis 2:16 that "You are free to eat from any tree in the garden; but you must not eat from the tree of the knowledge of good and evil for when you eat of it you will surely die."

If you are familiar with the Book of Genesis in God's Holy Word, you know "Then the Lord God made a woman from the rib he had taken out of the man, and he brought her to the man..." (Genesis 2:22)

Chapter 3 is referred to as "The Fall of Man." This scripture goes into detail about how the crafty serpent had a plan. He led Eve to believe that God was keeping something from her, and he placed doubt in her mind. He tricked her into taking fruit from the forbidden tree and eating it. Then she gave some to her husband; and he, too, ate the fruit.

The taste of the fruit from the tree of the knowledge of good and evil opened their eyes to their nakedness and sin. Then they covered themselves and tried to hide. (This sounds similar to how I tried to hide those hoeing mistakes.) But they heard the sound of the Lord God as he walked through the garden in the cool of the day.

When God confronted them, Adam admitted that they hid because they were naked, and that Eve had given him some forbidden fruit

to eat. Eve told the Lord that the serpent deceived
her.

Genesis 3:14-19 explains the burden (or
punishment) to Adam and Eve, and answers some
of our own questions. For example:

1) Vs. 14 - the curse for the snake to crawl
on it's belly and eat dust

2) Vs. 15 - God put enmity between snakes
and men; the reason snakes fear people and
people find snakes repulsive

3) Vs. 16 - the pain of childbirth. Eve
(women) would suffer pain in childbirth,
and desire for her husband who would rule
over her.

4) Vs. 17&18 - Because Adam sinned in
the garden, God told him: "Cursed is the
ground because of you; through painful toil
you will eat of it all the days of your life.
It will produce thorns and thistles for you
and you will eat the plants of the field."
(Some folks may read this as a reason for
being a vegetarian.)

5) Vs. 19 - "By the sweat of your brow
you will eat your food until you return to

the ground, since from it you were taken; for dust you are and to dust you will return." (Justification for cremation, perhaps?)

Then Adam and Eve experienced the first exile known to man when God banished them from the Garden of Eden to work the ground from which he (Adam) had been taken.

So after studying God's Word, we learn why we have thorns and thistles and hard ground to cultivate. Those stubborn weeds just keep coming back after we hoe them out, just as sin comes and goes in our lives.

We are ashamed, like Adam and Eve, when we identify our sin or try to hide it. But God is present with us through our, sins just as He was with Adam and Eve. If we accept Christ as our Savior, we may hear Him coming to us "in the cool of the evening." He may chastise us, but He will love and forgive us if we ask Him to do so.

The serpent "won his encounter" with Eve; but when God sent His Son Jesus Christ to die on the cross, His own blood became a ransom for our sin.

GOD WITH US

About ten years ago when my brother was the music minister for Enon Baptist Church, he planned and directed a musical program called "God With Us" that was written by nationally-known songwriter, Don Moen, and published through Integrity Music, Inc.

Michael was a wonderful music minister with a beautiful voice of his own. His leadership and encouragement helped the choir grow, and Enon was very blessed to have so many talented Christian singers. Some of the choir members sang their first solos, and discovered the gifts God had given them.

This musical contained the following titled songs:

"I Want to Be Where You Are"
"Overture Medley"
"Let There be Glory and Honor and Praises"
"Come Into His Presence"
"Crown Him"
"All We like Sheep"
"Be Strong and Take Courage"
"He is Faithful Medley"
"Blessed Be the Name of the Lord"

"How Great, How Glorious"
"Celebrate, Jesus"
"Jesus Is Alive"
"God Will Make a Way"
"Name Above All Names"
"No Other Name/All Hail the Power"
"Give Thanks"
"Crown Him"

These are some of the most beautiful musical tributes to our Lord and Savior. During all these years, I have continued to listen to this tape over and over again. These songs are based on scripture and have become part of my daily devotionals. They are so uplifting!

My favorite of these songs is "God Will Make a Way." The verses go like this:

> "God will make a way, where there seems to be no way. He works in ways we cannot see. He will make a way for me. He will be my guide, draw me closely to his side. With love and strength for each new day, He will make a way…He will make a way."

According to Don Moen, this song is intended "to give us hope in a hopeless situation." In the musical, this song is followed by two short stories that are spoken to music. Rather than using the stories from the tape, Michael had a married couple and me give our testimonies in less than 2-3 minutes.

It was quite a challenge to write that short summary, but I remember how special it was to be involved in the presentation. Being a part of this musical at a low point in my life showed me that God will indeed make a way.

Recently, I heard a Christian speaker say, "God will move heaven and earth to get us where he wants us to be (if we allow him to)." And the key answer there is that God is with us, as long as we want to be with him.
Some of the words to another of the songs say this so perfectly in my life as follows:

> "I just want to be where you (GOD) are, dwelling daily in your presence...I don't want to worship from afar; Draw me near to where you are."

> "I just want to be where you are in your dwelling place forever, take me to the place where you are. I just want to be with you."

"I want to be where you are, dwelling in your presence, feasting at your table, surrounded by your glory, in your presence that's where I always want to be…I just want to be…I just want to be with you."

(Repeat Verse 1)

"Oh my God, you are my strength and my song and when I'm in your presence, though I'm weak you're always strong. I just want to be where you are, in your dwelling place forever. Take me to the place where you are, I just want to be with you."

Recently, I broke my cassette tape and had to replace it with a CD. If I had been unable to replace this piece of music, I think I would have been sick at heart. If you need to hear some special uplifting Christian music, I encourage you to treat yourself to a closer walk with God through this powerful music.

"Emmanuel, God is with us and He shall reign forevermore."

O, WHAT A SONG!

A friend offered to take me to church the first Sunday in May. We visited once again at Trinity Baptist on Highway 601, and I amazed Donna by walking from the car with my rolling walker, and later in and out of a restaurant.

I was even more surprised, because each step I took was easier than any time in the past six years since the major multiple sclerosis attack. I didn't feel weak, I wasn't leaning on the walker, and I made it almost all the way to the front of the church. All of the aisle seats were taken, and I knew it would be impossible for me to step over someone else. I didn't want to have to ask anyone to move.

It was a challenge to walk that far, but I was glad I was able, because I haven't been "a back row Baptist" since I was a teenager. Besides I could see and hear better. It was a good thing because the pastor told us to look directly at him, and listen, because he had an important lesson from God's Word. The sermon title was: Jesus said, "You Must Be Born Again."

In the Baptist church, "born again," is also referred to as "being saved." Baptist beliefs are based on God's Word. The pastor's first reference was to Second Corinthians 6:1-2 that reads as follows: "As God's fellow workers we urge you not to receive God's grace in vain. For he says, 'In the time of my favor I heard you, and in the day of salvation I helped you.' I tell you, NOW is the time of God's favor, NOW is the DAY OF SALVATION."

The pastor also discussed Second Peter 3:9 which is covered in my study Bible as "The Day of the Lord." Verse 3:9 reads as follows: "The Lord is not slow in keeping his promise, as some understand slowness. He is patient with you, not wanting anyone to perish, but everyone to come to repentance."

The pastor proceeded to give several reasons why one needs to "be saved" today. First of all, we should not wait because God's Word says "TODAY IS THE DAY OF SALVATION." Another reason is that we ALL have an "appointment with death" and know not when we are scheduled to die.

He then proceeded to discuss "the judgment" and how there is no getting around death and the judgment. He also talked about the Second Coming of Christ (1 Thessalonians 4:13-18). In the Baptist church this is referred to as "The Rapture." He finished up talking about how real "hell" is and reiterated the importance of "being saved today by the grace of God."

This was a powerful message and the songs "We Shall See Jesus" and "O How I Love Jesus" were very inspiring, but the second verse of "Victory in Jesus" spoke to my heart more than anything else because of my disability. This has been one of my favorite songs since I was a little girl, and it was ironic that the last two churches I have visited started the service with this song. I had such a wonderful time of worship. When I got home, I called all my friends I could think of and warned them that they know I can't "carry a tune in a bucket;" but my heart said sing it to everyone you can, so here's what I sang:

> "I heard about his healing of his cleansing pow'r revealing
> How he made the LAME to WALK AGAIN and caused the blind to see.
> And then I cried, "DEAR JESUS,

COME AND HEAL MY BROKEN
SPIRIT," and somehow Jesus came and
brought
To me the victory...

O victory in JESUS, my savior, forever,
He sought me and bought me
With His redeeming blood:
He loved me ere I knew Him
And all my love is due Him,
He plunged me to victory
Beneath the cleansing flood."

Wow! "He made the lame to walk again,"
and it was my day, my week, my month. At least
four restaurants, churches, and then on Friday
finally walking in and out of the pool, and
swimming laps for the first time in six months.
This will help get rid of the pounds that restaurant
food puts on me.

I wish I could walk into the church every
time the doors are open, but that will happen only
if it is God's plan for me. For right now, I just
praise Him and give thanks for friends like my
two Donnas and Teresa who have taken me to
church several times. And thanks to Donna Fulton
for allowing the Lord to use her to help the "lame
to walk again" on this glorious day.

PROMISES, PROMISES, PROMISES

Have you ever made a promise you didn't keep? And if so, for what reason? Was time (or lack of it) an issue? Did it have to do with where you were? When you made that promise, did you really intend to keep it? And if you didn't intend to keep it, why did you say, "I promise?"

Promises are basically good intentions. One might say, "I really intended to…" or "I planned to but…" Sometimes it is said that the road to (wherever) is paved with good intentions.

The pavement on our highway of life is often full of potholes, or other abrasions. Our empty promises are just like unfilled potholes. These potholes create bumpy rides, and a series of broken promises results in unstable relationships.

As these thoughts about promises came to my mind, I remembered some of God's promises. A little book I once received as a gift is titled "Promises from God's Word." I searched the house over and finally remembered where the little book has been tucked away. In the introduction, one is reminded that this book of

Bible promises can be used for personal comfort, devotions, or even as a group Bible study. One hundred and fifty topics cover situations which most folks have experienced at one time or another.

Sometimes we view promises as stated facts and not necessarily pleasant ones. But sometimes facts just sound like promises. In 2002 when I had a major attack of multiple sclerosis (MS), the following facts sounded like promises that I prayed could be broken. Medically speaking, it appeared I would never be able to stand, walk, swim, or perform numerous other activities that most folks enjoy as a "given."

For five months through physical therapy and dedicated determination, I prayed and talked to God daily about the promises in His word. Finally one day in extreme pain and desire, I rose to a standing position at my dining room table. I knew then that prayers were being answered and healing was underway.

Six years later, I still cannot stand for long periods of time or without the assistance of a walker. But the ability to stand and transfer from the wheelchair to bed or bath, etc. is answered prayer like healthy people have never needed or experienced.

In the last few months since I have been able to attend church more often (and lost 25 pounds), I bought some new dresses. I have felt so blessed to be able to walk down the aisle with my walker to experience the presence of our Lord and Savior in His sanctuary.

It was such a delight to stand long enough to have some pictures taken to share with friends and family who live away from here. My young neighbor has been amazed at how tall I am when I stand. She had no idea how hard it would be for me to stand straight very long. I explained how I had once lost trunk control, and couldn't even sit up straight. For awhile, I had flopped around like a fish out of water.

As we talked, I thought back to my healthy teenage years, when I thought short girls were blessed, and that I was too tall and skinny. Oh, if I had only realized then how blessed I would feel to stand straight and tall now in the presence of short women.

Remember earlier when I said I was astonished where my prayers for story topics sometimes take me? The following Sunday after I started this story about promises, the opening song at Trinity Baptist Church was another one of my favorite old hymns. As the congregation rose to sing "Standing on the Promises," my heart began racing and I knew that I, too, wanted (and needed) to rise and sing what my heart was feeling. If you are not familiar with this song, it is as follows:

"Standing on the promises of Christ my King,
Thro' eternal ages let his praises ring;
Glory in the highest I will shout and sing,
Standing on the Promises of God."

CHORUS: "Standing, standing, standing on the promises of God my Savior, standing, standing, I'm standing on the promises of God."

"Standing on the promises that cannot fail, When the howling storms of doubt and fear assail. By the living word of God I shall prevail,
Standing on the promises of God."

(CHORUS)

"Standing on the promises of Christ
the Lord,
Bound to him eternally by love's
strong cord,
Overcoming daily with the Spirit's sword,
Standing on the promises of God."

(CHORUS)

"Standing on the promises I cannot fail,
Listening ev'ry moment to the Spirit's call,

Resting in my savior as my all in all,
Standing on the promises of God."

(CHORUS)

I was able to stand through the first three stanzas and choruses; and even though God hasn't blessed me with real singing talent for the enjoyment of others, He knew that I was standing on His promises and singing for His blessing.

I HAVE A SONG
I NEED TO SING

I felt very blessed when I was able to attend Trinity Baptist Church again. I don't get to go to church as often as I once did, because of having to depend on others for transportation. I miss those days, but I believe God has his hand in this... "And we know that all things work together for good to them that love God, to them who are called according to his purpose." (Romans 8:28)

Please don't get the wrong idea; I'm not complaining, and I don't want sympathy. What I do want is to make sure that those of you who are able, and have a way to go will be more thankful; and show your appreciation by praising the Lord when you enter His sanctuary.

This church is filled with a Bible-believing, soul-winning congregation, and I have felt the presence of the Lord every time I've attended. The pastor is very dedicated to bringing people to Christ, and travels around the country preaching at revivals.

Pastor Cox has an engaging way of starting his sermons, and a serious, but delightfully wry sense of humor. This particular day he made a statement that has stuck with me ever since. He said, "You don't sing if you don't have a song."

I have previously written about some of my musical experiences there, but I sensed, just as others in the congregation did, that the pastor was not literally talking about music, but rather about our personal relationships with Jesus, and the importance of sharing our love for the Lord with others.

Pastor discussed the scripture about the wise and foolish builders (Matthew 7:24-27). The sermon topic was "Build on Your Savior." Just as the man built his house upon a rock, it is important for us to build our lives on a relationship with Christ.

The pastor made some interesting points about how Jesus had POWER that was felt by the common people. (The religious leaders did not believe in the power of Jesus, or later, in his resurrection.)

He also pointed out how people who have "predicaments" are the ones who will "listen" when we try to "tell" them about Christ. Pastor

Cox also reminded us that sometimes those people, who are the "haves," think they don't "need" Jesus.

He shared some scriptures that showed predicaments that brought common people to Jesus. Some examples were: 1) A man named Legion who was demon-possessed (Mark 5:1-20). In my opinion, drugs and alcohol are examples of demon-possession in our world today. 2) Illness, or death of our loved ones, gets our attention just as the death of Jairus' daughter troubled the common people then. (Mark 5:20-24 and Mark 5:35-43)

There were some other incidents (scripture) like the woman with the issue of blood (Mark 5:25-34), the woman at the well, the paralytic man (Luke 5:17-26), and the death and resurrection of Lazarus. I glanced around and realized that others were just as amazed as I was at how much scripture Pastor Cox was covering. He had the rapt attention of the congregation, and God certainly uses him to bring the lost to the Lord.

All of these were perfect examples of the facts, just as they still are in our predicaments today. Jesus is the answer, and the only way to God is through our Savior. God can help us survive rough times. I know my life has been a "predicament" that the Lord has led me to share with others through writing or speaking. Praise be to the Father, the Son and the Holy Spirit!

One scripture he shared that was special to me was Mark 5:36 when Jesus said, "Be not afraid, only believe." Personally, this reminded me of why I do not live in fear; well, not as bad as some folks do anyway.

Pastor Cox brought the service to an end by sharing some of his own experiences in bringing the lost to the Lord. The church has a large bus ministry; and on his route, he had met a man and his young child who is in a wheelchair. The pastor asked the father if he had accepted Christ, and both the father and son admitted they had not. Pastor Cox then shared the plan of salvation and invited them to church.

The young man had told the pastor he had no clothes to wear to church, because their home had just recently burned down, and they lost everything. On Sunday morning, the young man and his child came forward and joined the pastor. The preacher eyed him up and down, demonstrating how he had done so the day before, and told him (and the congregation) that he had clothes in his closet that would fit this man. (Can you believe they both wore size 10 shoes?)

If anyone does not see the Lord in this, I encourage you to visit Trinity Baptist Church on Highway 601 close to Greasy Corner near Mocksville, North Carolina.

I've always said I can't carry a tune, but I had a song and felt God urge me to sing it to those who have just read this story.

MY CUP HAS OVERFLOWED

Finally, four weeks after carelessly breaking my foot, it was time to start standing and trying to learn to walk again. The morning after the doctor said I could start putting my weight on my foot, I stood up to get a saucer from an overhead cabinet. I was reminded of something I've wanted to share with others who maybe have never heard this song. It is called, "I'm Drinking from My Saucer Because My Cup has Overflowed." The song is sung by Michael Combs. It starts like this:

> "I've never made a fortune; probably too late now.
> Oh, But I don't worry about that much,
> 'Cause I'm happy anyhow.
> As I go along life's journey, I'm reaping better than I sowed;
> I'm drinking from my saucer 'cause my cup has overflowed."

This is how I've tried to explain my feelings during these difficult times. I am so blessed and have so much to be thankful for, even though a broken foot did set me back a bit. But there have been some small rewards to sitting. This particular morning, Woody, the redheaded woodpecker, joined the other birds at my feeder. I had just told a friend the day before, that I would love to have a woodpecker like we used to have at our home when my husband was living. I've had an abundance of cardinals, blue jays, finches, and doves to watch but no woodpecker until February 13th. My "bird-watching cup" certainly "overflowed" that day.

"Ain't got a lot of riches,
Sometimes the going's rough;
But I've got a friend in Jesus
And that makes me rich enough.
I thank God for all his blessings on me.
And the mercy that he's bestowed.
I'm drinking from my saucer,
'Cause my cup has overflowed."

This verse reminds me of the financial situation that so many folks have faced the last year or so. Some folks have lost so much, while others had so little to begin with. In these troubled times, it is difficult to know what decisions we should make about our financial future. I'm personally struggling with a decision as to whether to finance a conversion van. It would be the ideal transportation for me, my family, and friends, but is this a good time in these days of high gas prices and "rumors of war?" I need to pray about this, but I also need to remember that my cup overflows with the kindness of others who are willing to take me where I need to go. Folks are not available to suit my every whim, but someone is always there for the essential trips.

"Oh sure, I've been through some storms
and, yes, I'm sure
there were times when my, well, my faith
must have got a little thin.
But you know what it seemed like one day
all at once those dark clouds broke, and
that ole sun, she started shining again.
So Lord help me not to grumble and
complain about the truck rows I have hoed,
I'm drinking from my saucer, 'cause my
cup has overflowed.
And if I should go on living, if the way
gets steep and rough; won't ask for other
blessings 'cause I'm already blessed
enough. May I never seem too busy, oh
Lord, to help another bear his load; and I'll
keep drinking from my saucer, Lord,
'cause my cup has overflowed; my cup has
overflowed!"

The first time I heard this song was during a period of being "at the top of the mountain." I had just moved into my new home, my health was good, my family was healthy; and, I was traveling to speak for the Lord, and teaching a Sunday school class. This song impressed upon my heart that "my cup had surely overflowed," and I shared the song with others in my Sunday school class.

After the major multiple sclerosis exacerbation in July 2002, I wasn't listening to this music, and I'm sure that was one of those times when "my faith must have got a little thin."

In bad times, it is not God that has moved. When I'm not in church, reading the Bible, or other devotionals, or listening to music like this, it is easy for me to slide back to the period in my life when I was the one who had "moved away from God."

Well, I don't want to move away from my friend, Jesus. The writings of others, whether in verse or song, remind me of how, despite the storms of my life, my cup has overflowed, and I'm blessed to have a saucer from which to drink the overflow.

Readers often tell me how my faith inspires them, and they wish they could feel the way I do. My words do not compare with the poetic way that this song reflects the feelings of my heart. Listening to this song daily, as I read my devotionals, reminds me to praise God from whom all blessings splash over into my saucer.

STANDING TO SING

"I Stand Amazed in the Presence." Is that a song title or a feeling evoked by a song? Actually, it is both! Being able to stand to sing in the church sanctuary after so many months in the wheelchair, I knew it was God's amazing grace that had put me back on my feet long enough to sing three songs.

We were having a special rededication service of our recently remodeled sanctuary, and I felt strong enough to rise each time to sing. It is interesting that two of the songs on the program were as follows: "Amazing Grace, How Sweet the Sound" and "I Stand Amazed in the Presence."

I couldn't help trying to smile as I sang. Rising, standing, smiling, singing, all at the same time, were gifts from the Lord. (My husband used to say I couldn't "walk and chew gum at the same time." And that was when I was well!) But God can do as many things as He wants to do, all at the same time. It was a joyous occasion for me to sing praises to His name!

My ten-year-old grandson, Billy, made the rededication service even more special when he showed how much he was paying attention. The interim pastor asked each of us to bring him three names of people we would love and trust to lead our church during this period. Billy pulled on my arm to get my attention. By gesturing towards me and then the pastor, he indicated that he would give him my name.

How innocent Billy is to think I could assume such awesome responsibility! I had to explain to him that my health problems would not allow him to submit my name. I know Billy loves me, but it is a blessing to know he trusts me that much.

God certainly had his hand in my life at this service. Three times the night before, I had awakened to the sound of steady rain, and going to church had not looked too promising. (Those are the only times I miss the garage that everyone thought I should have built with my dollhouse.) But the skies cleared for a few hours, and gave me the opportunity to encounter these blessings.

It also blesses me how songs touch me at certain times in such a way. The songs, "Come Just as You Are" and "Open the Eyes of my Heart" are wonderful songs to lead one into personal Bible study and worship, in the morning. By the bay window at my dining room table, I can stand and sing to the top of my lungs, and no one knows how terrible I sound. But God's word says to "make a joyful noise;" it doesn't necessarily say it will be a beautiful noise!

A COVENANT RELATIONSHIP

How many friends do you have? How close do you need to feel before you consider someone a friend? How much do you want to know about a person before you become friends? Are acquaintances the same as friends?

Some of my "friends" ask where I get my story ideas, and there's an easy way to answer that this time. I was watching one of the preachers on television and his message was about friendships.

He had some interesting comments that came from God's Holy Word. It seemed to be a good time for me to think and write about this; so borrowing from his sermon, I will add my own thoughts.

Rev. Dollar views friendship as a three-tier level, comparable to the Old Testament scriptures that refer to the outer circle, the inner circle, and the Holy of Holies which was the part behind the curtain where only the high priests were allowed.

After listening to his sermon, I decided to review some of the friendships and acquaintances I have been blessed to have in my life. My "outer circle" has consisted of those who "know" me. Back when I was a stenographer in the Training Department in P-Building at Fiber Industries, my name was on my desk. Since I was the only woman in the building, many people "knew" me by name. Hundreds of people walked by my door every day, and I only knew a few of them.

Today, my outer circle is filled with readers who "know" me through my stories. I seldom meet most of these folks or hear directly from them; but I'm pleased to know "via the grapevine" that these folks "feel" as if they "know" me. Some of these people have done some really nice things for me even though we have never met.

My inner circle is filled with so many great friends (old and new) who bless me daily. Since I've been wheelchair confined, some of them call to check on me every day, or at least once a week. These friends seem to enjoy doing things for me every time I turn around. I'm on a lot of prayer lists for which I am very thankful.

In the center "Holy of Holies" circle, I have family, and friends who are like family, even if they are not blood kin. I am a blessed person who has a great deal of difficulty deciding who my best friend is, because all of these folks are so special to me in their own way. Because of lack of space, I can't begin to tell you all the amazing things these friends have done for me. Some of their acts of kindness seem small to others, but to me are extraordinary blessings.

Rev. Dollar discussed the scriptures regarding friendship. God established a covenant relationship with Abram (Abraham) that is referenced in James 2:23: "And the scripture was fulfilled that says, "Abraham believed God, and it was credited to him as righteousness," and he was called God's friend."

> In Ecclesiastes 4:9-12 we are told: "Two are better than one because they have a good return for their work. If one falls down, his friend can help him up. But pity the man who falls and has no one to help him up! Also, if two lie down together, they will keep warm. But how can one keep warm alone? Though one may be overpowered, two can defend themselves. A cord of three strands is not quickly broken."

In John 15:13-14, Jesus said, "Greater love has no one than this, that he lay down his life for his friends."

Most of us have never literally "laid down our life" for a friend. In a friendship, however, we all need to be "givers," not "takers." If you are involved in a friendship and you are always the one who does the giving, it may be necessary to reevaluate that relationship.

According to the preacher, "right friends are a blessing, wrong friends are a cursing." Sometimes if one has been hurt by a friend in the "holy of holies" circle, one often doesn't want to allow another person into their heart of hearts. For those of us who live alone, we are usually exposed less often to a love/hate relationship. And if one has been hurt, it's easy to withdraw into one's own shell.

A famous author once said, "No man is an island." God intended for us to have a covenant relationship with Him; and healthy friendships with others is one of His many desires for us.

Some folks are blessed with many friends, and I'm definitely among the most blessed. It's my desire to be a "giver," not a "taker," to make room in my inner circle and my heart for those who need a friend. One can't trust everyone like a "best friend," but a good relationship can take us to a new level; and with prayer, we can continue to be a blessing to others.

The following scriptures can help you learn more about God's view on friendship: "A righteous man is cautious in friendship, but the way of the wicked leads them astray." (Proverbs 12:26) "He who walks with the wise grows wise, but a companion of fools suffers harm. (Proverbs 13:20) "A friend loves at all times, and a brother is born for adversity." (Proverbs 17:17)

Are you a friend to the friendless? Are you willing "to be made willing" to be a friend to someone in need?

Jesus said, "For I was hungry and you gave me something to eat; I was thirsty and you gave me something to drink, I was a stranger and you invited me in, I needed clothes and you clothed me, I was sick and you looked after me, I was in prison and you came to visit me." (Matthew 25:35-46)

In today's wicked sinful world, it is sometimes hard for us to help strangers, but we should weigh opportunities to share God's word, and follow our heart.

BADGERING FOR JESUS

Badgering for Jesus…Is that what I was doing? Is that a bad thing or a good one? When we think of animals as pets, badgers are certainly not on our lists. Well, besides meaning a burrowing animal, *badger* also means to harass, chide, pester, cajole, coax, or wheedle. The following is my example of badgering for Jesus.

My new neighbor and I have become really close friends. She has taught me a new hobby (stamp art), and I have taken her on several windshield tours around Rowan County. Both of us have health problems and even take some of the same medications with similar side effects. It has been intriguing that we sometimes read each other's thoughts, or even finish the other's sentences.

We have read scripture and prayed together as we share food, our time, and our interests. During the cold winter months, we talked about going to church together in the spring. Debbie has not had a home church since moving to North Carolina, and I sensed that she has been searching spiritually.

March was not very encouraging for either of us, but finally April 10th arrived. It was a gorgeous sunny morning with no rain predicted, and the temperature was expected to be in the low seventies. I called early to invite Debbie to attend service with me at eleven o'clock. At first, she pleaded off and said she just didn't feel well enough.

"Ah, come on," I said. "It's a beautiful day. You might feel better if you get out of the house. Besides, going to worship service, being in the presence of the Lord in His house is where we need to be."

Debbie agreed with me, but was still hesitant. I think Satan was whispering in her ear. She didn't think she had the right clothes to wear; but saying that was useless 'cause God doesn't care what we wear; well, at least not if it is decent. She was afraid she might get sick and need to go to the bathroom. No excuse as far as I'm concerned. She doesn't know how many times

I've had to leave the sanctuary during service to go to the bathroom.

I told her someone would push us inside with wheelchairs, and we could sit near the back exit which is only a few yards from the restroom. Personally, I'm not a "back row Baptist," but I could sense her reservations weakening; however, she then asked about the temperature in the sanctuary. Since I am cold-natured and she is just the opposite, I explained that she would probably be comfortable.

That "still quiet voice" encouraged me not to give into her hesitancy. I sensed that it was important for me not to quit trying to convince Debbie to go to worship with me. I told her my son-in-law would be preaching, so finally she said, "Okay, I'll go." We agreed we should get off the phone and get ready if we didn't want to be late.

I believe Debbie was as comfortable in our beautiful sanctuary as a handicapped person can be. I think my friend realized that the pews are neither too hard nor too soft, that the air was neither too hot nor too cold. (Well, maybe not "just right," but close enough if one goes prepared with a magic scarf and winter gloves like I did.)

Debbie and I had an uplifting experience listening to the music. Leslie Davis, our pianist, performed a medley of hymns (Worship in Music); and her husband, Jesse, led the choir in special music, "He is the Rock." The organist, Charles Fulton, played "The Church is One Foundation" while the congregation sang. Wow, it was all so awesome! My son-in-law preached from Matthew 5:13 about how we are supposed to be the "salt of the earth." He made some good points about what Christ asks of us as Christians.

After church, we decided to go out to lunch with the assumption that I could find someone to help me get my wheelchair in and out. God provided one of my dearest neighbors coming out of the restaurant just as we arrived. Debbie and I were able to enjoy lunch together as we discussed our morning in the presence of the Lord.

By the time I drove into Debbie's driveway, we were both tired and physically hurting; but emotionally, we were energized! Debbie told me to write this story, and call it

"Badgering for Jesus." She said this thought had come to her mind as she hurried to get dressed after I called. Debbie said if I had not "badgered" her, she would not have gone to church with me. I told her that she is not the first person that I have "badgered for Jesus." Then Debbie said, "Oh, so this is your personal ministry, badgering for Christ." We had some great laughs which contributed to making me feel "a little salty." But I knew the only reason I didn't give up was because of that "still small voice" that kept telling me the right things to say to my thirsty friend. The glory belongs to our Lord.

GOD AT WORK
OVER AND OVER

I'm the most excited I've been in awhile. When I see God at work in my life, I'm so encouraged. I must be worth something in spite of my disability and shortcomings.

My new friend, Debbie, got me started stamping greeting cards. At first, I thought I would only make a dozen or so, and be through with that project. I told her I couldn't afford to buy the necessary articles, but she said she had ten years worth of material that she would be delighted to share with me; so our stamping friendship got underway.

I'm not very good at the stamping part, but I remembered how much I like to color. Debbie provided me with numerous colored pencils. Then I found out how challenging it is to match the colored articles to the beautiful papers which Debbie supplied. I think I have become addicted to coloring every evening as I listen to the television in the background.

Within a couple months, I had made several hundred cards. "Debbie, what are we going to do with all these cards?" I asked. "You will be surprised how many opportunities you will have to use them," she replied.

And she was right! God provided several ways. Once my daughter saw the results of my new hobby, she suggested that I sell the cards and use the proceeds for our upcoming youth mission trip. Her husband is the interim youth minister, and he was delighted to have another fund-raising project.

I wasn't sure if the cards would sell, but we ended up making over $250 for the youth. Debbie and I were delighted. We already believed that God had brought us together, and now we knew He was using us to help others.

After we sold all the cards we could, I still had over 200 and again found myself wondering what I could do with that many. Of course, we can use some for birthdays, anniversaries, etc., but we are still making more almost daily. Once again, Debbie told me not to worry.

She has been so delighted that I have found something I enjoy doing, and we both have been amazed at how easy this has come to me. My older daughter had always wanted me to find a new hobby, and little did we realize that God was at work laying out His plans for Debbie and me.

The "Art on Easy Street" project came along, and we investigated the possibility of earning some money for ourselves; but that project became too cumbersome for us with our disabilities, so we passed on it. (Later, we realized it was not God's plan for us to reap financial rewards for ourselves.)

Shortly after that, my daughter heard on the radio about a project involving greeting cards. A group from Winston-Salem was collecting cards to send to our servicemen and women overseas because they do not have a Hallmark store within their reach. Sometimes they like to have cards to send to their families and friends, but have limited access to purchase any.

I was so excited when I heard about this and couldn't wait to tell Debbie. She has been very sick and I knew this would be uplifting for her. Neither Debbie nor I have any family, or close friends, in the service today, but this would be the perfect use for all the cards we had made.

The only thing I was concerned about was the cost of mailing. I remembered that once when I mailed some used Christmas cards to the St. Jude's Ranch for Children some of my church members helped pay the postage, so I felt led to invite folks at my church to participate in this project.

I was telling all of this to the disability van driver, and another handicapped passenger heard the story. I had never met the lady, but before I got off the van, she pulled out a dollar bill and said she wanted to help pay the postage to send these to our servicemen. I could tell she was on a limited income and was reminded of the story in the Bible about the widow's mite. In Luke 21:3, Jesus said, "Truly, I say to you that this poor widow has put in more than all." No one but God and this sweet lady know how much she has that she can give away so freely.

This experience has enriched my life and when I got off the van, I told the driver to keep my change for the disability van service. After all, suddenly I felt really wealthy and in awe of how God uses us when we are willing to be used.

HE STOPPED THE RAIN

In the Old Testament in God's Holy Word, there is a story about how God answered prayer, stopped time, and added seven years to the life of Hezekiah. I wrote a story about how I felt God added years to my life during some rough times.

One weekend while traveling with a friend out of state to visit a loved one, all three of us experienced how God still answers prayers. On Saturday morning, Donna and I were praying that the expected rain would hold off at least until she could get me and my luggage loaded. We barely got damp.

As we traveled south on I-85, the rain switched slowly from a mist to a real downpour. Fortunately during our three-hour drive, neither of us had to get out in the rain for anything.

Nearing the end of our trip, we started talking about how we wished the rain would at least lighten up enough that we could get the scooter and me into my friend's house without getting soaked. We decided to share our wishes with God by breathing a short prayer.

Just as we turned onto the street where my friend lives, we looked at each other and at the sky. Then we smiled and gave thanks because God had stopped the rain. Debbie's brother was there to help get my scooter and me up two small steps.

After the work was finished, and introductions were made, Debbie said she also had been praying that God would stop the rain, or at least slow it down, until after we arrived. Donna left to travel a bit further to her sister's house, and again we prayed for her safe arrival there. About forty-five minutes later, we received a call that she had arrived safely in spite of the fact that the sky had opened up, and rain had poured down on her. (The Lord knew she could walk while carrying an umbrella.)

Debbie and I had a wonderful time stamping and coloring cards while Donna visited with her sister. Debbie has a tin roof, and all day and night we heard the rain and the wind. Donna called the next morning and said we should leave a little earlier because the storm was moving in faster than had been predicted. She said she would be there as soon as possible. An hour later, she had not arrived, and the rain was beating down hard once again.

I said, "Oh, Debbie, let's pray once more that God will deliver her safely and stop the rain again while we get all this stuff loaded up." (Because of Debbie's generosity in sharing her card supplies, there was more to carry back than we had arrived with.)

In less than ten minutes, we looked at each other and sighed in relief. Just as Donna arrived, the rain had ceased, and once again we discovered that the prayer of three believers had been answered.

With the help of Debbie's son, and after hugs and tears, we were back on the road once more. We drove all the way to Kannapolis in hard rain and heavy, slow traffic. Donna and I talked about our visits and the weather. We prayed that God would help us get off the interstate and travel the remainder of the way safely. We figured we would request one more time that He stop the rain.

Did you count the number of times God answered the fervent prayers of three believers?

Just "do the math" and add one more time because he stopped the rain again just before we reached my development.

All these answered prayers reminded me of Noah and the Ark, and Moses and the Red Sea. Some skeptics will say, "Oh, those were just coincidences." But the word coincidence really means "God at Work" in my vocabulary; and if you don't want to believe and pray, then you won't see answered prayer in the same way the three of us did. One has to believe in God to receive answered prayer.

Before the day was over, snow moved in and the three of us were safe and sound in our own homes. The following day, I was told there had been a terrible accident which shut down I-85 for eight hours. People were removed from their vehicles as they ran out of gas and had no way to stay warm. Some were moved to shelters. Had we not left earlier than planned, we could have been involved. (I dread the possibility that someday I will be one of those folks freezing on the interstate.) When I arrived home, I had prayed once again that I would not be without power; and I woke up to a toasty warm house with plenty of light, food, and water.

After reading this, do you believe in answered prayer, and God's ability to "stop the rain?" If not, let's get together for a Bible study.

MY BARNABAS

I had the privilege and pleasure of
attending a youth program my grandchildren
participated in at their church. It was a blessing to
finally get to watch my older grandson play the
drums to Christian music. My other grandson
took part in a skit, and my granddaughter sang
with the group.

My son-in-law is the youth minister and
has a large group of students from 6th to 12th
grades. The youth group has been on many
mission trips where they   learned valuable lessons
about loving their neighbors, and helping others.

After the service, Pastor Wayne shared his
appreciation to the youth minister and the young
folks for the service on which they had worked so
hard. There were several adults, including the
choir director, who had spent a lot of time helping
those kids prepare this worship service for the
Lord.

Anytime youth are involved, adult
volunteers are needed. Pastor Wayne discussed
this by asking volunteers to "come alongside" and

help support the youth minister, and the young people in all of their activities. Because of my disability, I'm unable to do so, but I was reminded of a Bible study in which I was once involved.

In studying the Book of Acts, I learned about Paul's many mission trips. A fellow named Barnabas was Paul's first traveling companion. The name "Barnabas" means "son of encouragement," but in that Bible study. we were told that Barnabas also means "one who came alongside." God had chosen Barnabas to support Paul in his mission trip.

I realized this was similar to what Pastor Wayne was encouraging the congregation to do where the youth are concerned. I thought of my own position as a servant of the Lord. He has given me an opportunity to be "Barnabas" to many other disabled folks.

My name, Linda, may not mean "son of encouragement," but he has given me opportunities to be an encourager to others who need help in their spiritual and physical journeys. I have an Aunt from Panama; and when I was a little girl, she told me that in Spanish "Linda" means "beautiful." I certainly never considered myself beautiful, but I pray that others see "beauty" in my attempt to reach them in service for Christ.

During the years that I traveled speaking for Christian Women's Club, I guess I was "kin" to Paul in my mission work, and God brought a wonderful friend into my life; Gerri Holshouser became my "Barnabas." She was such an encourager as she sat time after time listening to me share with others how God has been the anchor in the storms of my life.

Are you a Barnabas in someone else's life? Are you willing to be an encourager to others? Has God called you to "come alongside" someone who has circumstances similar to your own? If you feel that you were called in service to the Lord, then don't hesitate to be available to help youth and others as needed.

Service to the Lord should be the mission of all Christians.

A RELATIONSHIP
LIKE NAOMI AND RUTH

I only have daughters, so I will never have a daughter-in-law. But of course, I was one once upon a time.

Recently while studying the book of Ruth in the Bible, I was reminded of the origin of the passage, "Where you go, I will go, and where you stay, I will stay. Your people will be my people and your God my God."

Contrary to how it sounds in the wedding vows, it doesn't just mean we're making this pledge to our husbands; most of the time, we're marrying their families as well, especially our mothers-in-law. Actually, Ruth made this commitment to her mother-in-law, Naomi, not to her husband.

After a two-day honeymoon, my husband, Joe, and I moved in temporarily with his mom and dad. I wish I could say that his Mom and I were as close as the biblical Naomi and Ruth, but it took several years, and the birth of my first daughter, for us to become comfortable with each other.

Joe was the youngest of six children, and some would say he was a mama's boy. To me, at seventeen, he was my "man," and I may have resented her not wanting to untie the apron strings.

Likewise, she may have resisted me edging my way in between them. Irregardless, once my first child was born, I developed a deeper understanding for my mother-in-law's feelings.

As time passed, she and I became very compatible. She taught me many things in the kitchen, and helped a great deal with my children. As Naomi advised Ruth, Mrs. Beck also gave me lots of good advice.

I, in turn, tried to help her in different ways, particularly when age and ill health began to take its toil on her. I know that she and I both developed a lot of respect for each other.

When she became a widow, Joe and I tried to fill some of the void in her life; as a widow myself now, I realize there was only so much we could do. We certainly couldn't replace Joe's dad.

I'm extremely thankful to God that Joe outlived his mother. Mrs. Beck lost one adult son, and that was very heartrending for her. The biblical Naomi not only lost her husband, but also two sons, so she ended up with her daughter-in-law, Ruth. If Mrs. Beck had lived to see Joe suffer with cancer, she would have been devastated.

I find it somewhat ironic that my own mother passed away shortly before my oldest brother died. I'm thankful, too, that my mama didn't have to experience losing her oldest son, though she had buried her first two children many years ago at childbirth.

Sometimes it's hard for us to understand why things happen the way they do, or when they do. For those of us who are Christians, however, we can see God's purpose and plan for our lives when we study the Bible.

The name, Ruth, means "friendship" and over a period of years, Joe's mom and I cultivated a friendship that I remember with great satisfaction. Just like Naomi and Ruth had to travel, make plans, and glean the fields, Mrs. Beck and I had to hoe some rows to weed out those early problems in our relationship, but the love for the same young man was worth the effort.

My daughter lives in her grandmother's
house now, and she enjoys reliving memories of
her grandmother. I pray that someday when her
two sons marry, she will be like Naomi in the lives
of her daughters-in-law.

PAIN CAN TAKE YOU DOWN

I almost forgot that pain can take you down. One morning when I was transferring to the shower, I hit my leg against the wheelchair. As the pain shot through my body, my knees buckled, and I started down. Fortunately, I was right at the handicapped bar and was able to stop myself from going all the way to the floor. I said a prayer of thanks, because I didn't have to call for help in my "birthday suit."

Physical pain can be a real handicap. I have several friends that have chronic pain from multiple sclerosis or fibromyalgia. The pain from this can put them to bed for hours, or even days. Those who enjoy good health and have never experienced chronic pain have no empathy for these folks and sometimes even have no sympathy. I have little patience for folks who condemn those who suffer from physical or emotional pain. Remember, physical pain can affect one's emotional state of being as well.

Another friend of mine has back trouble and when her back "acts up," she is forced to stay in bed lying as still as possible in order to deal with the pain. Sometimes it takes several days for this to pass.

I understand that pain. In 1976 when I developed a staff infection after a thymectomy, I found how difficult it was to even rise to a sitting position. Turning over was a definite "no, no." Even during the healing process, I lived with chronic pain for over a year.

Several corrective surgeries later taught me that no major surgery is pain free. With the possible need for two other surgeries facing me down the road, I try to change the subject when this comes up in conversation.

There are various medications that we can use for pain. Some of these are for temporary use, while others are habit-forming, but may be necessary to make the pain bearable.

Then there are times when what gives us peace with the pain is prayer, and knowing that others are praying for us. Having someone to talk to that just listens and cares is a blessing from God.

I was reminded of a story I read by the Methodist preacher, Charles Allen. He shared a story with his congregation about a little girl who went on an errand for her mother.

> She was late coming back, and her mother asked why it took so long. The little girl said that a playmate of hers down the street had fallen, and broken her doll. She told her mom that she had to help her friend. The mother wondered what she could have done to help mend the broken doll. The little girl's reply was precious when she said, "I just sat down and helped her cry."

Wow, what a friend! I have some friends like this. They have all been answered prayer for me over the years, and I praise God for putting folks like this in my life. I know there are some folks who don't have as many friends as I have, and some have no family, or maybe none nearby. To these folks whom I know, I hope God will enable me to just sit down and listen. I'm reminded of the song, "What a Friend We Have in Jesus," and that's the kind of friend I wish I could be. Maybe I could at least be the handicapped rail that helps them stop the pain from taking them all the way down.

REMEMBERING TO FORGET
CAN BE A VALUABLE SKILL

Can one forgive without forgetting? I'm not sure. I told someone recently that God has blessed me with forgetfulness. Now there are times when that blessing is frustrating. When I'm trying to remember something, forgetfulness can be a real pain. And yet, there are some things I'm glad I'm able to forget. My daughters claim I have selective hearing, and remember only what I want to remember. (There may even be a smidgen of truth to that.)

Recently, I read about a conversation someone once had with Clara Barton, the founder of the American Red Cross. He reminded Barton of a vicious deed someone had done to her many years before. She acted as if she had never heard of the incident.

"Don't you remember it?" her friend asked. Barton replied, "No, I distinctly remember forgetting it." That's the best response I've ever heard.

There are so many people suffering emotionally because of things in their past that they haven't been able to forget. Painful childhood memories haunt some people throughout their lives and cause unlimited sorrow and grief. Some people are unable to cast these demons from their minds. Physically, they continue to exist, but emotionally, they're unable to move beyond the hurt and pain.

Corrie Ten Boom was never able to forget her family's experiences in the concentration camp during the Holocaust, but with God's help, she was eventually able to forgive one of the guards who had tortured her and her sister, who died in the camp.

I read a book about an amnesia victim who didn't remember anything about her family or life prior to being hit by a car. And we hear more and more about people who have Alzheimer's Disease. Of course, no one wants to be a victim of either of these types of memory loss.

But wouldn't it be wonderful if we could all be like Clara Barton and distinctly remember to forget the things we need to forgive?

THE SAMUEL PRAYER

Have you ever prayed, "The Samuel Prayer?" In my Bible, First Samuel 3:1-21 is referred to as "The Prophetic Call of Samuel." But recently, I heard a preacher refer to this chapter as "The Samuel Prayer." (If you are not familiar with this chapter of the Bible, I encourage you to review it before you read any further in this article.)

On the other hand, if you have read the book of First Samuel, then you are aware that Samuel was the son the Lord granted to Hannah and Elkanah after Hannah prayed because "the Lord had closed her womb."(1 Samuel 1:6) Eli, the priest, had seen her mouth moving, but did not hear her prayer so he thought she was drunk. She explained how she had asked for a son, and promised if her plea was answered that she would "give him to the Lord all the days of his life and a razor shall never come on his head." (1 Samuel 1:11)

The Lord later granted Hannah's request; Samuel was born and after he was weaned,

Hannah took him to the temple and left him in the care of Eli, the high priest. (1 Samuel 1:19-28)

In chapter 3:1, "...the boy, Samuel, ministered before the Lord under Eli." (During that period of time, "word from the Lord was rare and visions were infrequent.") In my Bible, it says Samuel was no longer a little child; the Jewish historian, Josephus, places his age at 12, or a little older. I found this intriguing because when I was growing up, twelve years old was often referred to as "the age of accountability." (Oh, I feel another story coming on.)

I know you must be thinking that one can read all this from the Bible, but bear with me as I set the stage for "The Prophetic Call of Samuel." Samuel and Eli were retiring for the evening. (3:2-3) In verses 4-10, the Lord called Samuel and Samuel replied, "Here I am." In verse 3:7, we are told "Now Samuel did not yet know the Lord; The word of the Lord had not yet been revealed to him."

Samuel thought Eli was calling him, but Eli discerned that the Lord was calling the boy, and after the third call, Eli told Samuel to go lie down and if the Lord calls, he should say, "Speak, Lord, for your servant is listening." (Verse 3:9)

After listening to the pastor preach from the book of First Samuel, and studying in my Bible, I realized that what makes this episode important in our lives (or in my life today) is when the Lord calls out to us; do we say, "Here I am."

Are we ready to answer God's call in our lives? Will we be available to serve where he wants us and follow his will for us? Many of us hesitate because we don't think we have the ability, but there is a message that reads "God doesn't want our ability, he wants our availability." Some of us fear what God will call us to do... as I might pray that God won't call me to go to Siberia...Brrr (or anywhere that is colder than here.)

After Eli instructed Samuel to lie down, the Lord called as at other times, "Samuel! Samuel!" And Samuel said, "Speak, for your servant is listening." Listening to the pastor as he shared how he has heard the Lord call, "Wayne! Wayne!" and he replied, "Speak, for your servant is listening" took me to that place which brought this story to fruition.

I prayed and said to the Lord, "Speak, for your servant, Linda, is listening." And though I did not hear the Lord's voice, the Holy Spirit encouraged me to share my vision of Samuel's experience as if it were happening in my life or the lives of other Christians (and possibly even some non-Christians).

In Verse 3:11, the Lord said to Samuel, "Behold, I am about to do a thing in Israel at which both ears of everyone who hears it will tingle." Did this story get your attention? Are your ears tingling? Are you ready to say, "Here I am, Lord" if God calls on you? Have you been able to discern God's plans for you life? Are you willing to share your beliefs with others, even when they may not really believe as you do? Are you "willing to be made willing?"

People often ask where my stories come from, but when I say "from the Lord," I can sense some doubt; folks tend to give me too much credit. It's always interesting to me that people, places, and things come into my life in such a way that I personally do see God at work.

For example, I'm unable to go to church every week like I used to, and this has given me opportunities to hear some really good preachers on television. I arrange my schedule to fit the times of their sermons. But sometimes there is a period when there's nothing on TV that I am interested in watching. God gave my daughter the insight to bring DVD's of their church's Sunday morning service to me. The sermons like this one, speak to my heart, and that "still small voice" says "Share it;" so I hope you have heard the Lord call you by name and that you, too, will reply as Samuel did: "Speak, for your servant is listening."

THE POWER CUBE

As I was crawling out of bed one morning, this article came to mind. Electric wheelchairs these days are called "power chairs," and mine is charged with a portable "power cube." The power cube is plugged into the wall receptacle behind my bed. Each night I have to plug the cord from the cube into the receptacle on my chair, and then flip the "on" button.

Having been accustomed to plugging my three-wheel electric scooter directly into the wall receptacle, this power cube was answered prayer. Since I have to transfer directly from the chair to the bed, I had been concerned about the location of the wall sockets and the length of the power cord, and how I would know when the chair batteries were fully charged. The designers of the chair and the power cube had anticipated these kinds of needs, and there was an answer to each of my concerns.

The chair should be charged every night; and when first plugged in and turned on, the cube shows a red light which indicates the "need to be charged."

During the night, when one sees a solid red light and a flashing green light, this indicates that the chair is eighty percent charged. Later, there will be only a solid green light indicating "full charge," and the chair is ready to go. I flip the switch, unplug the cord from the chair, transfer, and start my day.

Now, the designers didn't tell me how the lights had to start all over every time I have to get up during the night to go to the bathroom. They didn't tell me what to do when my power was out for five days. The chair itself does, however, show red (needs charging), yellow (caution), and green (fully charged). The Woodleaf Volunteer Fire Department took care of charging the chair with a generator during the ice storm. They were like angels who knew all the answers and were sent from above with a message.

Some of you are probably yawning by now. You may think this is like reading the boring manuals that come with items we purchase, or those insurance policies, we are supposed to read. I'm sure many of you might wonder why an article like this would be in a book about faith.

It was interesting to me because the Holy Spirit showed me how this compares to our Christian walk. Just like the power chair, we, as Christians, need to be "charged" daily. My electrical source is God above, and my portable power cube is His Holy Word, the Bible.

When our lives are in the "red light zone," it's time for us to stop and examine our relationship with the Heavenly Father. We need to delve into His word, pray and fellowship with other Christians in Bible studies and social gatherings where we can communicate our desires, views, and concerns.

The stationary red light shows we are interested Christians, and the flashing green light is an example that we are not fully charged "in our Christian walk." We need more knowledge of God's word – His commands, His promises, His love, and His forgiveness.

There are so many words in the Bible that are sometimes hard to understand. We need to research and study the scriptures that contain words for which we are uncertain of the meaning.

Attending Bible studies, worship services, or studying on one's own, will provide the "electrical charge" needed to help us get to the "solid green light stage" which shows we are "good to go."

Then it's time for us to get out of our beds, off our couches, and out of our comfort zones to share the Good News with others. God gives each of us different spiritual gifts with which we can achieve these goals to His glory.

The particular morning that inspired this article caused me to see the electrical power, the power cube, and the power chair as God the Father, the Son, and the Holy Spirit. I felt charged to write this story to express my beliefs in the Trinity, to share my love and need for God in my life, and to suggest how others can feel God's presence in something like a power cube.

My knowledge of His word is limited, but nine years of dedicated reading and studying the Bible, has given me that peace for which so many folks are still searching.

Not everyone may need devices for the handicapped as I do, but we all need the Lord and His word. I challenge you to plug into the power source (God) and allow yourself to be fully charged! If your memory is as bad as mine, you may feel you are at eighty percent or less, but God loves you and He blesses our efforts; sometimes with a full charge in the middle of the night.

RECHARGING
OUR SPIRITUAL BATTERIES

Every time I turn around, something needs new batteries. After twenty-one months, my power chair needed two of these. These are the large expensive kind, but thankfully are covered by Medicare so someone came to my house to take care of this.

One chilly morning, I discovered the batteries were dead on the remote control for my gas logs. Fortunately, I have a wall switch and was still able to get warm. Shortly after that, the batteries for my TV remote quit working. (My grandsons were lost; they couldn't channel surf.)

For many months I was unable to stand up on my bathroom scales and when I finally could, the battery was dead. Are you bored to sleep yet? You're probably thinking we all have problems with our batteries needing recharged or replaced so why is she droning on about her batteries.

Well, allow me to add some food for thought. Sometimes I think my "spiritual" batteries need recharging. Have you ever felt that way? Sometimes circumstances drain our "spiritual batteries." How can we recharge or replace these?

Reading and studying God's word, praying and listening to Christian speakers and music, can "recharge our spiritual batteries." One way might be to learn about the will of God. In a recent sermon, Dr. Charles Stanley provided the following information.

God will show His will consistent with his promises in Psalm 32:8: "I will instruct you and teach you in the way you should go; I will counsel you and watch over you." Psalm 16:11 reads: "You have made known to me the path of life; you will fill me with joy in your presence, with eternal pleasures at your right hand."

In Second Timothy 3:16-17 Paul says, "All scripture is God-breathed and is useful for teaching, rebuking, correcting, and training in righteousness, so that the man of God may be thoroughly equipped for every good work."

Sometimes God's will is revealed to us through circumstances. Other times, our conscience helps us to determine God's will, and common sense can help us to recharge our spiritual batteries.

In his sermon about the will of God, Dr. Stanley advises that if we don't have peace about something, we should not do it. He says peace is "God's umpire." We should watch what God does in our lives when we obey Him.

God is the power source that will revitalize our spiritual batteries if we allow Him to. Instead of asking what we can do about our lagging spirit, we should ask God what He will do to help us recharge our spiritual lives. Notice I said we should ask "what He will do," not "what He can do" because God can do all things. A good summary thought for this is "it is not believing God can, it is believing that He will."

IN THE SHELTER
OF THE MOST HIGH

There is an interesting story that some of you may or may not have ever heard. In the biography of Jimmy Stewart, the famous actor, we learn about his service to our country as a fighter pilot. He fought numerous dangerous battles, and returned safely home as a decorated Brigadier General.

So you probably know or may be kin to a lot of loyal Americans who served their country and returned safely. But unless you've heard what Jimmy's father placed in his pocket just before he left, your curiosity is probably about to get the best of you. (Don't you love happy stories?)

We were told that his father owned a hardware store, but all that really matters is the degree of faith he had. The elder Mr. Stewart placed a copy of Psalm 91 in his son's pocket, and instructed him to keep it there during his service to our country.

I've forgotten how long the actor served, but he returned to a wonderful career as one of the very popular actors whom most everyone loved.

He was married to one woman the rest of his life, and raised her children as his own.

I would like to encourage the folks who have friends or family in the military to make a copy of this Psalm and place it in the pocket over the heart of these military men or women. Then pray, and reread this Psalm when you need a lift and encouragement for their safety.

PSALM 91

He who dwells in the shelter of the
Most High will rest in the shadow of
the Almighty. I will say of the Lord,
"He is my refuge and my fortress, my
God, in whom I trust."
Surely he will save you from the
fowler's snare and from the deadly
pestilence. He will cover you with his
feathers, and under his wings you will
find refuse; his faithfulness will be
your shield and rampart.

You will not fear the terror of night,
nor the arrow that flies by day, nor the
pestilence that stalks in the darkness,
nor the plague that destroys at midday.

A thousand may fall at your side, ten
thousand at your right hand, but it will
not come near you. You will only
observe with your eyes and see the
punishment of the wicked.

If you make the Most High your
dwelling –even the Lord, who is my
refuge –then no harm will befall you,
no disaster will come near your tent.

For he will command his angels
concerning you to guard you in all
your ways; they will lift you up in
their hands, so that you will not strike
your foot against a stone.

You will tread upon the lion and the
cobra; you will trample the great lion
and the serpent.

"Because he loves me," says the Lord,
"I will rescue him; I will protect him,
for he acknowledges my name.

He will call upon me, and I will
answer him; I will be with him in
trouble, I will deliver him and honor
him with long life will I satisfy him
and show him my salvation."

In the Book of Daniel when King
Nebuchadnezzar became angry with Shadrach,
Meshach and Abednego, he told them if they did
not serve his gods or worship the image of gold he
had set up, that he would throw them into the
blazing furnace.

In Daniel 3:17 & 18, they replied: "If we are thrown into the blazing furnace, the God we serve is able to save us from it, and He will rescue us from your hand, O King. (Daniel 3:17) "But even if He does not, we want you to know, O king that we will not serve your gods or worship the image of gold you have set up." (Daniel 3:18) The king got very angry and threw them into the fire, and had them stoke the flames so high that it killed the soldiers as they got close. But the king leaped to his feet, and asked his advisers "Weren't there three men that we tied up and threw into the fire?" They replied, "Certainly, O king." (Daniel 3:24) He said, "Look! I see four men walking around in the fire, unbound and unharmed, and the fourth looks like a son of the gods." (Daniel 3:25)

And just as in Psalm 91 and the Book of Daniel, God is able and there for our soldiers; he can be their refuge, their dwelling place in the "fiery war" if they seek him with their hearts. And even if they have Psalm 91 in their pocket, our soldiers may pay dearly with their bodies, or even their lives, but God is able to give them eternal salvation in His dwelling place.

GOD GAVE ME TIME

Hidden deep in the recesses of the Old Testament in the Bible (God's Holy Word) are some interesting stories that I never remember being taught as a child.

In 1993 after my husband's death, I decided I was going to read the Bible through every year so I would have more knowledge of the contents. Sometimes, however, no matter how much we read, certain events don't quite register with us until the Holy Spirit speaks to our heart, or when a preacher speaks or writes on that particular subject.

The first example for me was when "The Prayer of Jabez" was on the best seller list, and I heard a service about Jabez asking God to expand his territory (First Chronicles 4:9-10). I've written before about how discovering those verses and prayer expanded my own personal territory.

Well, recently I was reminded of the story about Hezekiah's illness (Isaiah 36-39; 2 Kings 18-20; 2 Chronicles 29-32). (This is one of those stories I don't remember from my childhood.) It's also one of those sections in which I must have dozed off while reading, because I had never given any personal thoughts about these chapters.

This is that section where I don't know how to pronounce a lot of those foreign sounding names. (Personally I've come to believe that in the privacy of my own study, God won't be as concerned about how I pronounce the names as He will be concerning whether I'm studying His word or not.)

If you have never read about Hezekiah's illness (especially those of you who have health problems), I encourage you to read about this in those chapters previously noted. I heard this story mentioned by a minister on television, and he talked about how God "added 15 years to Hezekiah's life when he was at the point of death."

Hezekiah had prayed as he "wept bitterly," and asked the Lord to remember how he had "done what was good in the eyes of the Lord." (Isaiah 38:2-3) Having seen Hezekiah's tears and heard his prayer, God stopped the sunlight (Isaiah

38:4-8), restored Hezekiah's health, and added time to his days on earth.

Some of you may be wondering why I'm telling this Biblical story. Well, it is that time when the Holy Spirit spoke to my heart, and reminded me of how God has dealt with my numerous illnesses. In 1976 when I nearly died from a staph infection, I prayed for enough time to at least finish raising my two young daughters. There was much pain, sadness, and more episodes of bad health, but God answered those prayers and here I am, still living 33 years later.

In 2002 the major multiple sclerosis exacerbation took so much away from my body, and I was given dire predictions about the future, but I prayed that I would get well enough to return to my new home. Now six years later, I sit here in the shade in my beautiful yard. Yes, the house looks worse from the wear and tear of wheelchairs and scooters, but God gave me more time.

I'm not sure why God has rewarded me with a longer life when he took my husband away at the young age of 47. I just continue to thank and praise Him for the blessings I've received. In

Isaiah 38:9-20 after his illness and recovery,
Hezekiah writes in a poetic way what I now feel in
my heart after studying this Old Testament
chapter.

Isaiah 38:9-20 NIV
A writing of Hezekiah king of Judah after his
illness and recovery:
I said, "In the prime of my life must I go
through the gates of death and be robbed of the
rest of my years?"
I said, "I will not again see the Lord, the
Lord, in the land of the living;
no longer will I look on mankind, or be with those
who now dwell in this world.
Like a shepherd's tent my house has been
pulled down and taken from me.
Like a weaver I have rolled up my life, and
he has cut me off from the loom;
day and night you made an end of me.
I waited patiently till dawn, but like a lion
he broke all my bones; day and night you made an
end of me.
I cried like a swift or thrush, I moaned like
a mourning dove.
My eyes grew weak as I looked to the heavens. I
am troubled; O Lord, come to my aid!"
But what can I say? He has spoken to me,
and he himself has done this.
I will walk humbly all my years because of
this anguish of my soul.
Lord, by such things men live; and my
spirit finds life in them too.
You restored me to health and let me live.

Surely it was for my benefit that I suffered such anguish.

In your love you kept me from the pit of destruction; you have put all my sins behind your back.

For the grave cannot praise you, death cannot sing your praise;
those who go down to the pit cannot hope for your faithfulness.

The living, the living – they praise you, as I am doing today; fathers tell their children about your faithfulness.

The Lord will save me, and we will sing with stringed instruments all the days of our lives in the temple of the Lord.

As I was typing these verses on the computer, I was led to the line that says: "Surely it was for my benefit that I suffered such anguish." It was like seeing "the writing on the wall" as it answered the question, "Why me, Lord?"

It is amazing how studying God's word in the right place at the right time speaks to our hearts and answers our questions. I encourage you to open your Bible and spend time with the Lord.

GOD HASN'T MOVED

So much of the time we don't realize why things happen the way they do in our lives, but if you are a Bible reading believer, you can find the answer. For those of us who face each day with a handicap, our faith and knowledge of God's word can at least give us "that peace that surpasses understanding."

But sometimes when things turn for the worse, or we lose a loved one, we begin to doubt like Thomas did in John 20:24-30 after Jesus' resurrection. We question "Is God here?" "Why did He take my loved one?" "Why am I the one who has this disability?" "Does He still love me even if I have sinned, or if I am mad at Him?" "Why didn't He answer my prayers when I asked for healing (mine or someone else's)?"

People often ask where I get the ideas to write stories like this. Other than the main fact that God has led me to share my experiences through writing and speaking, things sometimes just take place, and a story will almost write itself.

Early one morning, I started to transfer from my recliner to my power chair to go to the bathroom. When my feet touched the floor, I knew something different was happening in my body and I nearly fell. As I made the other necessary transfers, I almost fell twice; and, my feet felt so heavy like they were no longer kin to the rest of my body. The next day I nearly fell twice getting in and out of the pool.

As soon as I got home, I called for an appointment with my neurologist. He could tell I was not doing as well as I was the last time I had been there, but reminded me to never assume that everything that happens in my body is from the multiple sclerosis. (This is a reminder to all of you who have MS.)

He ordered some tests and we discussed other issues, but that is not really what this story is about. Jim and Lou, a couple of my Christian friends, were kind enough to take me for one test, and then I introduced them to Hap's for lunch. (They agreed if you have never been there, you better go while you're able.)

We always have great conversations and sometimes they are about the Bible, our faith, and our personal beliefs. We were discussing how many people were on Noah's Ark, and I mentioned that the answer is in the Old and New Testaments. None of us could remember exactly where it is located, but I promised to call them when I found the answer.

After they left, I picked up my Bible and started waving the pages from the back forward, and it stopped at First Peter 3. My eyes fell down the page where I had underlined verse 20 that said "eight in all were saved through water, and this water symbolizes baptism that now saves you also…." (If you have a desire to know more, read verses 7-22.)

Turning directly to this page was like several incidents that I have written about. God guided my hand and helped me write this story after a long dry spell of that proverbial "writer's block."

So many of you may be thinking, "Why does she feel that this is important?" It's not really that I think it's important, but I like to play

Bible Trivia when I have a willing opponent. (Especially if I think I can win…Ha! Ha!)

Now allow me to get to the meat of this story. Since I broke my foot in December, I had not been standing or trying to walk since about two weeks before this episode. I had only been to the pool twice and had been successful until this episode happened. I had some other important issues with which I was trying to deal (like wanting to sell my house, and move to town where I would have more access to transportation), and other doubts and decisions I needed to make. (Have I been a "doubting Thomas?") Well, I did say if God wanted me to sell my house, He would send me a buyer. I also said He would do so in His time, not mine. Now, where's my faith?)

As I was trying to pray after this last event, I knew I was not allowing the "Holy Spirit to intercede" for me. I told the Lord that I knew He has not moved, but perhaps in the past few months I had moved mentally, emotionally, and spiritually. (My doctor later described this as "seasonal distress disorder" because I changed so quickly when spring arrived.)

Looking back at the recent events which have happened, I realized that the diagnosis of osteoporosis, controversy over medications, and other personal issues have caused me to allow some things to override the time I used to spend in God's Word and His presence.

I knew that making and recycling cards for our soldiers was a patriotic and Christian act, and that God had provided the opportunity. But because I enjoy doing it so much, and wanted to reach so many soldiers, I began to allow it to consume my time, even to the point of hurting my wrists and hands.

And then there have been so many nice compliments, and it has been suggested I should start selling the homemade cards. Well, since I could certainly use the money, I think that would be okay, if I keep it in the proper order.

Nothing, not health issues, friends, family, hobbies, or even jobs, should close the door to our hearts and our relationships with our Lord and Savior, Jesus Christ. God hasn't moved, have you?

THE LORD NEVER CHANGES

It is amazing how one major change in one's life, sets the stage for other differences. If one is brave enough to open a new door and step out of their comfort zone, life can offer new challenges and adventures.

The greatest adventure of all is when one decides to invite Jesus into his/her life. In Second Corinthians 5:17, the Bible describes this as follows: "Therefore, if anyone is in Christ, he is a new creation; the old has gone, the new has come." I discussed this in a service for children once, and used an old table that had belonged to my grandmother. The antique table had been refinished, and demonstrated how something old could become like new; just as change occurs when we open the door of our hearts to Jesus Christ.

In Revelation 3:20 the Lord says, "Here I am! I stand at the door and knock. If anyone hears my voice and opens the door, I will come in and eat with him and he with me."

Once we have established this relationship with our Lord and Savior, those "major changes" often lead to small "incidental changes" that are important to each of us individually, even though they may or may not be to anyone else. After the major multiple sclerosis attack in 2002, and my new card ministry for the soldiers, I have become more reclusive. Excessive cold, or heat, can be detrimental to those with MS, so I have spent more time inside than I ever have in my life. The Rowan Disability Transportation Service only allows me two days a week for appointments, etc., and I rarely go out at night since I quit driving.

Most of the time we don't know what plans God has in store for us, or even if they are His plans, but after a series of unexpected events, I knew it was time for some changes. My brother's daughter-in-law had become a makeup coordinator, and needed some customers, so I decided to get rid of all my old makeup and start fresh. We had fun experimenting with colors and getting to know each other and, I had a new friend. I learned about eye makeup, which I rarely had ever used.

So once again this "antique old Nana" is a new me. When I turned sixty in October 2007, little did I know that some delightful changes were in God's plan for this child of the King. So many changes in the past have been negative, rather than positive. It has been encouraging to experience the rebirth of shopping, eating out with friends, and finding a new purpose.

All of our lives are filled with changes; some sad, some happy, or sorrowful, costly, or complex. We have to learn to deal with change in a positive way if we want the inner peace that our Father God offers us.

There is one change that we don't have to be concerned about. God is unchanging. In Malachi 3:6 He says, "I the Lord do not change." And Hebrews 13:8 reads: "Jesus Christ is the same yesterday and today and forever." Our Lord and Savior Jesus Christ will never need a makeover, new clothes, or an expensive refinishing job. He is there in the good and bad times…always there, never changing.

RUNNING OUT OF TIME

Do you find yourself wondering about how fast time is zipping along? My friends and I frequently discuss this in one way or another. My family often relates time to the 16 years since Joe's death, the girls' weddings, and the births of my grandchildren. I, of course, also relate back forty years ago to the birth of my oldest daughter, and later the arrival of my youngest daughter.

Hallie Renee was two on 3/24/06, and I especially wonder how she grew as fast as I aged, since the 2002 major multiple sclerosis exacerbation. The recovery period seemed long and drawn out as I spent day after day reading, watching TV, and working puzzles; and now it seems I spend days not being able to accomplish all I want to do.

Due to health problems and medications, I find myself wasting minutes (or is it hours?) snoozing away. Alas, this is causing me to miss precious time with my baby granddaughter. I had been keeping her one morning a week, but when she started walking (or is that running?), several close calls took away those "Monday's with Hallie Renee." Common sense, and the importance of her safety, must outweigh the desires of my heart.

But how much time is left? I have been visiting at a church, and the Sunday after I started writing this article, the pastor's sermon was called "Running Out of Time." The verse he was referring to was Romans 13:11 which reads "And do this, understanding the present time. The hour has come for you to wake up from your slumber, because our salvation is nearer now than when we first believed."

Are we running out of time to bring others to an understanding of God's word? Are we, as Christians, going to allow books and movies like the DaVinci Code to cloud the judgment of unbelievers?

Are we willing to let the Holy Spirit use us to "win souls for the Lord." (It makes some people uncomfortable when one discusses the plan of salvation or "being saved".) Yet, we continue to allow actors and actresses to influence us in what we believe or do not believe.

I don't know about everyone else, but sometimes I feel like I am "running out of time" to read, to write, or to do all I want to do to help others learn the lessons I have learned the hard way.

The pastor told about a young boy who left home one morning, and neither he nor his parents knew he would have an aneurysm and not return home. Fortunately, that child was raised in a Bible believing church, and this gave his parents the peace they need to help them through this tragic loss. No one knows just why the Lord called that child home just as he has so many others.

Another church close by had a sign that read: "God changes lives faster than you can change lanes." Thinking about how fast time ran out for these parents, I thought of my own personal testimony. I did not know one morning as I walked into my new home that I would not "walk" into it again for a long time.

This article seems to be "changing lanes," but I'm writing what I feel the Lord is telling me to write. One other thing I have learned over the years is about anger and forgiveness. Do we realize that when we leave somewhere angry that we may never have a chance to apologize or ask forgiveness? Sometimes harsh words are hard to recall before time runs out for all parties involved. (Believe me I know because my personal opinions have made others angry faster than I can transfer from my recliner to my wheelchair, and I've become pretty adept at that.) But I thank God that in reading His word, I have come to seriously believe what He says about "never let the sun go down on your anger." "Being right" does not necessarily allow us another day or another opportunity to seek forgiveness.

Sometimes if we swallow our pride, we can ask someone to forgive our actions or words even if we don't think we were the one in the wrong. Unfortunately, sometimes even when we seek forgiveness, the other person doesn't accept things unless they get their way.

But once again, time is running out on all of us in one way or another. I'm sixty years old, and everyday I hear of so many younger folks than me that have passed away. To me it is important that I act on whatever I feel God tells me to do, whether it is simply apologizing, laying aside my anger or offering to share the plan of salvation with others through my speaking or writing. (If you are uncertain about the "plan of salvation," the following passages are referred to as "The Roman Road" and may help you study God's word. Romans 1:16, Romans 3:23, Romans 6:23, Romans 5:8, Romans 10:9-13.) Everyday I pray that what I say or do will be pleasing to the Lord, even if I step on the feet of sinners like me.

UNTIMELY LOSS

Time is slipping, slipping, slipping into the future. Where have I heard that? Was it a song...a poem? I don't remember, but it is certainly taking place in my life. January 2008 is almost over as I write this article.

One might wonder why I am dwelling on time. Well, the 15th anniversary of my husband's death (2/26/93) and the birth of that precious baby boy (Billy) who filled that empty space in my heart was 4/18/93. I remember how sad I was when they laid him in my arms, and I thought of my husband who would not be there to help raise his grandson. At first, I felt nothing other than sadness, but the little fellow (who is now taller than I am when I stand up from my wheelchair) stole my heart, and helped dissolve the sad emptiness I had experienced.

This article is for those who have lost a "soul mate" or gained a grandchild. A lot of you are familiar with my history as a wife, mother, and Nana. I'm sure many of you had more years with your mates than I did with Joe (27 years), so your period of "singleness" may have been much longer than my 15 years and you could probably write your own story.

I guess I just want to reach out to those who are in the early stages of grief; that period of time when long days and sleepless nights tire your body and confuse your minds. Those endless questions of "why, when, where, what and how" keep you wondering about the future. Then there are those long periods of dwelling on the memories of the past and those "dead zones" when one wonders if his/her life ever will be set upright again.

During this time of one's life, everyone else can tell you what you "could do," "should do," or "shouldn't do," and the main topic is generally "Don't move too quickly, or you will regret it later."

There's no question that I made some mistakes, but I have never regretted selling my home and moving closer into town. (If I had been old enough, and the senior housing units had been available then, as they are now, I believe I would have moved to one of those.)

I spent nine years paying rent in an apartment that most folks would say was a waste of money, but since I was a "disabled widow" at the young age of 45, some of my choices were limited. The biggest advantage was that I had daily access to a swimming pool for water aerobics, and my health improved immensely.

When rent went higher than seemed comparable, I did move back to the country, and had a small house built. I was driving by then so all was well, but the major MS flare-up just four months after I moved in turned my life upside down again.

I have written so many stories about all my "roller coaster rides" that some folks may be tired of reading them. I'm sure though that some of you are either new to Salisbury or to the YMCA, and possibly never read The Salisbury Post, Senior Savvy, or Primetime.

I'm full of "good advice," "bad advice," or "no advice," but my little doll- house has become a sanctuary that many troubled people love to visit. God has given me a concern for others who face situations like mine, and has enabled me to share how His Word and His love has helped me become a survivor. He is the potter and we are the clay; He can mold us and make survivors out of those who are willing to put our losses in their proper place, and move on making a "new" life.

Sometimes others will be judgmental and not always favorable to our decisions, timing, or new relationships, but we need not fear or worry about the thoughts of others. Scripture in Psalm 68:5 tells us that (God) is a father to the fatherless, a defender of widows (widowers), and is in His holy dwelling.

One of my favorite verses is from Second Corinthians 1:3-4: "Praise be to the God and Father of our Lord Jesus Christ, the Father of compassion and the God of all comfort, who comforts us in all our troubles, so that we can comfort those in any trouble with the comfort we ourselves have received from God."

I have come to realize that this is one of the missions God has given me. The song, "Sanctuary," which follows gave me the idea of a name for my home, and a good friend had a sign made for me. So if you need the comfort that

God's word has given me, call me; and if it is God's will, maybe I can help you find "that peace that surpasses understanding." Then you can find your own sanctuary.

SANCTUARY
"LORD PREPARE ME TO BE A SANCTUARY
PURE AND HOLY, TRIED AND TRUE.

WITH THANKSGIVING, I'll BE A LIVING
SANCTUARY FOR YOU.

WHEN HE COMES IN SHOUTS OF GLORY
AND OUR TIME ON EARTH IS DONE
HOW I LONG TO HEAR HIM SAYING
FAITHFUL SERVANT, WELL DONE.

REPEAT

I NEED TO SHINE,
NOT WHINE

It just ain't like it used to be. And I am
sad! Am I whining or complaining? Yeah, I am.
I hate to disappoint my readers by writing a
negative sounding story, but there is a saying,
"The truth shall set you free." (In fact, that saying
is embedded on the front of the newspaper
building and it comes from John 8:32 in the Holy
Bible.) Some days I need the freedom to share the
truth, without losing the respect of others.

God knows my heart, so there is no
pretension with him. My family has to deal with
our losses in our own personal ways and my
grandsons miss the things that used to be. But
even they have come to understand how my health
limits the things we can do together now. Their
Nana has the same heart, but a somewhat different
body.

This particular "down" day was one of two
days the boys and I had spent at the new YMCA
pool during their Mom's lunch break. For the first
few years of their lives, we spent a major part of
every day during the summer in the outside pool

having fun in the sun. I helped teach the little guys to swim, even before I learned how.

This last multiple sclerosis exacerbation has caused me to get colder in the water and in air-conditioned places, so I was watching from the sideline as the boys played in the water for 45 minutes.

When I moved from the apartment, we still had access to an outdoor pool at the Health and Fitness Club, and I sure miss my "home away from home." My plans had been to spend part of most every day there in the summer, just as I had done in the apartment pool. Unfortunately, the pools there are not handicapped accessible so that opportunity, too, has passed with this exacerbation.

I watched the elderly ladies come and go in and out of the water. I'm sure that most of them have their own health problems, but I covet their independence; their ability to still walk and drive. I reminded myself that many of them either have no grandchildren, or that perhaps they rarely see them. I know in that respect I am blessed; but this particular day that didn't make me less jealous. I needed some extra prayers to remove the sin of covetousness from my heart.

I know I have come a long way in my recuperation, but the truth is I have a long way to go. Several weeks of intense pain caused me to question the future truths I might have to face. Then I spent some time dwelling in the past, and reviewing all I have lost.

This all took place in the same week that I had taken a friend to see my old home, and showed her pictures of the way my husband and I had landscaped our yard; the house and yard no longer look like we had planned and Joe's been dead since 1993. Unfortunately, while looking at the pictures, we came across the one of him taken just before he died. My sadness deepened when I thought of all we missed together. Then twice that week I dreamed of Joe and it was so real until I woke up, and was reminded that he is gone and I am alone.

Well, I'm doing all those things I advise others not to do. I'm living in the past, struggling with the present, and dreading the future. The truth is, right now I am a slave to negativity. I'm not exhibiting a Christ-like attitude to others or myself.

David Ring, a Christian Evangelist, was born with cerebral palsy, and has endured a lifetime of health problems. I heard him speak several years ago when he appeared in Salisbury. He is a remarkable man, and has a great philosophy. His theory is that we should "Shine, and not whine." I pray that I can be more like David Ring.

Now that I've shared the truth, I am free to be me, as I am, and not as others often perceive me to be.

BELIEVERS OR UNBELIEVERS

I've said before that there are two kinds of people: givers and takers. One morning I woke up cold at 2:45 am and had to get up to adjust the thermostat. The first chilling thought that came to my mind was about two other kinds of people - believers and unbelievers. The second thought that made me shiver was something I once heard a preacher say… "God does not hear the prayers of an unbeliever."

Which are you? Do you believe in God the Father, the Son and the Holy Spirit? Do you have faith that God is in control. Do you believe He is holding you in the palm of His hand? Have you accepted Jesus Christ as your Savior? Do you believe God's word?

As these thoughts came to my mind while I was turning the thermostat up, I knew I had to transfer to my recliner instead of going back to bed. I guess since I cannot kneel on my knees, this recliner is my "prayer chair" because it is where, with God's help, I usually write first drafts of my stories.

God gave me these three paragraphs and then as I became cozy and warm, He must have sprinkled "sand" in my eyes, because I fell back to a restful sleep.

If I wake up by seven in the morning, I enjoy watching Rev. Creflow Dollar. This particular morning his message was the second part of a series, "The Power of Prayer." He mentioned a book entitled, "Reasons People Fail to Receive Healing." I immediately realized some folks would say this was a coincidence, but I knew it was an amazing act of God that would be part of this story. I wish I could have ordered these materials, but the cost was beyond my means. I opened my Bible to see where God would lead me.

The previous evening, I had received an email from a friend who recently had serious surgery. She went into that surgery not expecting any complications, just as I did in 1976 when I ended up with a staph infection. Her healing has not been successful and she is bitter and angry with God.

I had not heard from her for a season, so I called and left a message. In her email reply after telling me some negative events, she said: "I also did not want you to tell me that if I believe, God will fix it; or He may or may not. I'm pretty sure by this time he ain't doing anything. I still wonder how you can have all of that faith, especially after all of the crap that has happened to you."

Once again, I sent her a note of encouragement that day. I continue to pray that she will study God's word and become a true believer. During bad times, we have to walk in faith, and never permit mental pictures of failure. We cannot experience the "fullness of joy," unless we let every thought and action become an affirmation of our faith.

In John 16:23&24 Jesus said: "In that day you will no longer ask me for anything. I tell you the truth, my Father will give you whatever you ask in my name. Until now you have not asked anything in my name. Ask and you will receive, and your joy will be complete."

My friend went on to say: "This is no fun for me or for my husband to have to drag me around in a wheelchair, when I used to be able to walk and run; and personally I don't know how you stand it."

I've tried to explain this before; I can "stand it" or "accept it" (disability) because I am a "true believer." I realize that there are so many others who are worse off than either my friend or me. Even after my remissions and relapses with multiple sclerosis, if I focus on my Father God, I can be healed in His timing though I may not become the 100% woman my friend longs to be.

She finished her email saying, "The only thing I can tell you for sure, living without being able to walk is not my idea of living. I absolutely WILL NOT be stuck in this wheelchair for the rest of my life."

I have a great deal of empathy for my friend, but it concerns me that she may be an unbeliever. Until she studies God's word and accepts his plan, she will never really "believe" she "can be healed." Like Doubting Thomas in John 20:29 Jesus said, "Because you have seen me, you have believed; blessed are those who have not seen and yet have believed." Because I have "believed without seeing," I have been blessed.

So many disabled people need to refocus on becoming "believers" and thank God for what we do have: two eyes, two ears, two legs, two hands (or even one of each) a mind, husbands (or wives) and families. We need to concentrate on what we've gained, rather than what we've lost. Many of us have pain and all kinds of inconveniences, but we also have opportunities to use our limitations to develop a personal relationship with our Lord and Savior Jesus Christ, and then share our beliefs with others.

And when my friend and others like us do this, we can come to the same realization that Joni Eareckson Tada did when she finished her book, "The God I Love." Her closing statement was "There are more important things in life than walking." And I certainly know that to be the truth!

THE PRAYER OF FAITH

I love how my Women's Devotional Bible (NIV) has each chapter divided by sub-titles that quickly catch my eye when I am searching for an answer in God's Word. Under the heading, "The Prayer of Faith," the following scriptures caught my attention and, henceforth, this article was born.

James 5:13-16: "Is anyone of you in trouble? He should pray. Is anyone happy? Let him sing songs of praise. Is anyone of you sick? He should call the elders of the church to pray over him and anoint him with oil in the name of the Lord."

What is faith? Faith is belief. Do you believe in the power of a prayer of faith? When you are happy, do you "sing" songs of praise to the Lord? My belief here is that folks like me who have no musical talent can "sing" praises to the Lord through speaking or writing (and maybe in the shower.)

Prayers of faith have been very important in my life because without my Christian beliefs, it would have been very difficult for me to have survived the heartaches and pains that I have faced. After the multiple sclerosis attack in 2002 when my toes would not even wiggle, I was told I would never walk again. My family, friends and I were deeply troubled.

Some members from my church came to the hospital to pray for me. They asked if I believed in the power of the "anointing with oil in the name of the Lord." I was familiar with scripture about prayer of the sick, and anointing with oil, but I had never really considered it a personal blessing that could be administered to a sinner like me.

I guess I thought it was only intended for "special chosen servants of the Lord." With the study of His word, I came to realize that all of us who have accepted Christ as our savior are his saints. Would it make a difference, if these fellow believers anointed me with oil? Did I have enough faith to believe this would help heal me? At that time, I was so mentally and physically in the depths of self-doubt, that I was willing to try almost anything.

But being anointed with oil required faith that if God wanted to heal me, He would be able to do so. Accepting the anointing, meant I had to work with the Lord to develop a plan of attack that would free me from that "self-doubt."

I was reminded of a couple of my favorite scriptures. From the Old Testament there is the one I claimed back in 1994:

> "But those who hope in the Lord will renew their strength. They will soar on wings like eagles; they will run and not grow weary, they will walk and not be faint." (Isaiah 40:31)…and in the New Testament Philippians 4:13 which reads, "I can do all things through him (Christ) who gives me strength."

During these past five years of mountains and valleys, Satan has tried, as he did in the Book of Job, to crush my spirit, to hinder my progress, and to cause me to doubt God. But in James 5:15-16 God's word reads:

> "And the prayer offered in faith will make the sick person well; the Lord will raise him up. If he has sinned, he will be forgiven. Therefore confess your sins to each other and pray for each other so that you may be healed. The prayer of a righteous man is powerful and effective."

UNHEALTHY DISCOURAGEMENT

I know at least twenty people personally who have some serious health problems and we all have days on which we feel worse than other days. Often when we have a really bad day, we tend to forget that others have suffered even more than perhaps any of us have. I think on days like this it is good to have a support group or at least the ear of one friend that can and will listen!

My friends and I talk about all the problems we have had, now have, or someday may have. Sometimes we get discouraged with the repetition of falls, pain, and then the occurrence of new symptoms that puzzle and worry us. Those of us who are Christians know that God's word tells us not to worry, but Satan tries to intervene and make us blame God for our troubles.

Recently I was reading an interesting book about tragedy in two devout Christian families, and the manner in which they faced their problems really spoke to my heart. They referred to different scriptures so I went back to my Bible to refresh my memory.

It seems quite often here lately, the Lord has led me to the Old Testament for the basis of several of my stories. In the Book of Kings 17-22 and 2 Kings 1& 2, we learn about the prophet, Elijah, and his dedication to God's work.

Elijah, like so many of us with health problems, became discouraged when things didn't go just the way he wanted them to. In his adventures, we learn about the discouragement of the widow of Zarephath (1 Kings 17:7-24)) who had barely enough food for her and her son.

And then we read about Obadiah (1 Kings 18:1-16) who was a devout believer in the Lord. Obadiah became discouraged because of his fear for his life. But in spite of his fear and discouragement, he followed the orders of the Lord through the commands of Elijah.

Sometimes for those of us with disabilities, it is difficult to hear God's voice through scripture but when I went back to reread this section of the Bible, I knew God had his hand in it. I had been spending time with a new friend who is so discouraged that we both had realized she needs a better understanding of God's word; and we hope to start a Bible study in my home for others with disabilities.

I know I can only lead a Bible study or bring someone to a relationship with our Lord and Savior if it is God's will for me to do so. But that particular day when I opened my ear to the discouragement of two friends, I knew that God was present. As I tried to speak for the Lord, he did not give me one word I needed and I became frustrated, and discouraged that maybe I didn't clearly understand how God planned to use me.

I began praying that I could be the comforter that would bring my troubled friends to that "peace that surpasses understanding." A few hours later as I shared the events of my day with my friends, Jim and Lou, I asked "What is the word I am searching for here?"

It was like plugging into an electrical socket when they reminded me that the word I wanted was "Emmanuel – God with us" and I knew Emmanuel had been a guest in my home that day.

I had never before discerned how God provides a "prescription" for those of us who become discouraged, but the following came to my attention in my Women's Study Bible.

1. We should get enough rest. (1 Kings 19:5)
2. We need to eat healthy foods on a regular basis. (1 Kings 19:6)
3. We must spend some quite time with the Lord. (1 Kings 19:9)
4. And after all this, we must then "go" and "do". (1 Kings 19:15)

If you are easily discouraged or plagued with health problems, I encourage you to study God's word. If you are unable to understand it alone, then get involved in Bible study or a church of your choice.

After Elijah listened to and followed the commands of the Angel of the Lord (vs.19:5-12), then the word of the Lord came to him:

(Vs. 11): The Lord said, "Go out and stand on the mountain in the presence of the Lord, for the Lord is about to pass by."

Then a great and powerful wind tore the mountains apart and shattered the rocks before the

Lord, but the Lord was not in the wind. After the wind there was an earthquake, but the Lord was not in the earthquake.

(Vs.12): After the earthquake came a fire, but the Lord was not in the fire. And after the fire came a gentle whisper."

Perhaps if you apply this scripture in your own discouragement, you may hear the gentle whisper of the Lord.

IS THERE ANYTHING GOOD
IN BAD HEALTH?

Does anything good come out of having a health problem? Well, most of us would rather not have to find out. But in Romans 8:28, the Bible says: "And we know that in all things God works for the good of those who love him, who have been called according to his purpose."

A lot of people, especially unbelievers, wonder exactly what is meant by "things." Most of my adult life has been wracked by various health problems and some folks wonder where I have found "good" in any of it.   I guess I could not have felt any "good" in the pain, the wheelchair, the doctors' visits, or hospital stays, if it were not for my faith in God and the study of His word. This led to writing and speaking about my personal relationship with Jesus Christ. And that has all been good for me, and according to some others, good for them also. Sometimes I see myself as a present day Job. At one time, everything seemed so right and good about my life; but then the health problems changed everything. I adjusted and readjusted so many times, just to find out that now I have severe osteoporosis, especially in (of all places) my right wrist.

If you've read my stories over the years, you know I used to hoe in red clay, pull weeds in my gardens, clean, sew, type, and write. Then for the past three years, I've made thousands of cards for our soldiers and some for my friends.

Now in the process of finally getting my stories ready for publication, I've needed a little extra money to take care of the finances. Over time, I've sold a few cards and donated the money to church functions, or paid to mail cards and buy supplies. Recently, I made a birthday card for a lady in the "Red Hat Society" and thought perhaps she might buy some of those cards. But it turns out that she is also a stamper.

Okay, okay, you probably wonder where all this ties together; sometimes it takes a lot to tell a story. With a broken foot and a diagnosis of osteoporosis, my foot was so swollen that the doctor sent me to RoMed for three days of "compression therapy" (oh, and it worked wonders.)

I've been there in past years for physical therapy; two ladies and one fellow remembered me. They've been so nice to me, and I used to work with the mother of one therapist. I remembered that her mother belongs to the Red Hat Society so I asked if she might want to buy some cards. This gal told me to bring some on my next visit and she would find out.

As it turned out, the other lady there is also in the Red Hat Society and as soon as she saw the two cards, she wanted me to bring all that I had ready and some samples of my other cards. She said someone else might show them in her gift shop. Well, I had several hundred cards to sell and a book almost ready to send to a publisher. I had been so frustrated with my swollen foot, but if I had not needed medical attention, I would not have found a place to sell my cards.

Now, ain't God good even in the bad times; well, certainly to those of us who love Him.

ARE YOU GUILTY?

"If you are arrested for being a Christian, would there be enough evidence to convict you?"

My friend, Evelyn, always knows just the right thing to say when I need to hear it. We were talking about someone who told me not to bother praying for her because there is no God. Ouch! In my nearly 60 years, I've only had a couple occasions when people questioned the existence of God in my presence.

Most of these remarks were made by people who have severe health problems that have gotten worse instead of better. People who are suffering severe pain are often angry with God, their doctors, and even their families and friends.

If others don't say what the sick person wants to hear, or do what is needed, feelings get hurt. (I'm sure I've hurt my families' feelings when I complain about my loss of independence.)

I am a Christian and I will not deny God. I will listen to the problems of others, share my feelings and beliefs, but I will not alter my belief to please someone else.

I explained to my new acquaintance that
her lack of belief was even more reason for the
prayers of Christian friends. So one might wonder
what any of this has to do with that opening
quotation. Allow me to share some thoughts
about what evidence is proof of being a Christian.

In Matthew 28:18-20 Jesus presented the
"great commission" to his disciples "to go and
make disciples of all nations…" Since that is one
of his commands to his followers, how could I
dare not at least try to reach others in his name
(even if they don't want to be reached).

I believe if I were arrested for being a
Christian, the fact that I try to tell others about
Christ through speaking or writing would certainly
be on the evidence list to convict me.

So what else would convict me? Let's see,
do I go to church? Well, I used to try to go every
time the doors were open, but now my disability
causes some problems there. However, I've
learned that going to church is not what made me
a Christian.

In Matthew 18:20 Jesus said, "For where
two or three come together in my name, there am I

with them." Sometimes my home has been a sanctuary for troubled friends, and I believe these folks would testify to my Christianity.

One of my friends said that I have been like "a light that dispels the darkness" in times when she has needed comfort. I'm sure there are some times when I "step on toes," but I try to use scripture to reach those who are in such pain. One day a very sweet lady overwhelmed me as she looked directly in my face and said, "I can see Jesus in your eyes."

Space will not allow me to share all the spiritual blessings I continue to experience when I speak to others about God's word and will in my life. Without my stories of illness, heartache, and the new adventures that resulted in the last fourteen years of my life, I could not have become the speaker/writer that God has planned for me to be.

In Second Corinthians 1: 3-4 Paul wrote, and God has taught me, about comforting others and this became another of my favorite scriptures: "Praise be to the God and Father of our Lord Jesus Christ, the Father of compassion and the God of all comfort who comforts us in all our troubles, so that we can comfort those in any trouble with the comfort we ourselves have received from God."

The lady, who said there is no God, has visited now and asked me how I remain "so upbeat." I told her she might not like my answer, but she wanted to hear what I had to say. I explained to her that I am a Christian and that in studying God's word, I have been able to turn my troubles over to Him and continue to enjoy the blessings that exist outside of the sorrows.

Had I remained bitter and angry with God through heartache, several illnesses, and the loss of my husband, I could not have become a comforter and friend to others.

Several people have said that I have comforted them and they wish they had the "peace" I have. I like to remind them of Jesus' promise in John 14:27: "Peace I leave with you; my peace I give you." That peace he gave me is stated so clearly in The Serenity Prayer: "God grant me the serenity to accept the things I cannot change; courage to change the things I can; and wisdom to know the difference." I like to encourage others to think about this, memorize the prayer, and put it into action. Would these thoughts, beliefs, and actions be evidence to my Christianity?

Sometimes folks wonder what good it does to pray when the results are not what they requested. But in Matthew 6:5-15, Jesus teaches what we refer to as "The Lord's Prayer" and in verse 10 he says, "thy (God's) will be done."

Some of us forget that we are His disciples and should pray for His will to be done rather than our own. Christians, who turn their backs on God because He didn't answer their prayers in their own will and way, will lose out on the blessings He has for them in other ways.

In Jeremiah 29:11-13 the Lord says, "For I know the plans I have for you; plans to prosper you and not to harm you, plans to give you hope and a future. Then you will call upon me and come and pray to me, and I will listen to you. You will seek me and find me when you seek me with all of your heart."

When we are victims of illness, we might wonder "why" and "if" our illness was in God's plan for us. I can't answer that for others, but I try to share my beliefs about how God has used my illness that I might help other people cope with the negatives in their lives. When I nearly died in 1976, I just prayed that God would enable me to go home and raise my daughters. I lived through an extended illness, raised my daughters, and it appeared to be answer to my prayer; but in reality it was God's will because He knew He had future plans for me.

When I look back at some of the major prayers that I lifted up to God, I can see that, as it says in Philippians 4:13, "I can do all things through Christ who gives me strength." And that "strength" has gotten me through illnesses and helped me remain the Christian God desires me to be. As Christians we must trust and obey and have faith that God will hear our prayers. Trust, obedience, and faith may be more evidence used to convict us as Christians. I surely hope I'm found guilty.

THE SINNER'S PRAYER

It seems that an article I wrote for the Faith Page left at least one reader wondering what I meant when I referred to "The Sinner's Prayer." She could not find anywhere in the Bible where this was mentioned.

People from different denominations worship God in different ways. The reader quoted a lot of scripture that she thought I needed to study, and some of this scripture applies to the prayer in question. Contrary to the reader's doubts, I have read and studied all the verses to which she referred. In fact, I have read the Bible through several times in the past sixteen years.

I grew up in the Baptist Church, and examples of the Sinner's Prayer are included in our church literature. I guess I never really thought about how this might be confusing to those of other denominations. We are all sinners, even though we don't always want to admit that.

As Christians, we know that even Jesus' disciples asked him to teach them how to pray. The Lord's Prayer is found in Matthew 6:9-15. In this well-known prayer, we ask for forgiveness, and that is one part of "The Sinner's Prayer." Other parts of this prayer include: acknowledging that we are sinners, asking for forgiveness, repenting of our sins, and inviting Jesus to come into our hearts and lives.

It is such a simple answer to how we obtain the key to eternal salvation. In John 14:6 Jesus answered, "I am the way and the truth and the life. No one comes to the Father except through me. If you really knew me, you would know my father as well. From now on, you do know him and have seen him."

God then sends the Holy Spirit to guide us in our lives and we become one of God's saints. This is what Baptists refer to as "being saved." This is a simple statement that is often misinterpreted by those of other denominations. Comments like "I got saved," or "I was saved," refer to the times Baptists feel that the Holy Spirit spoke to us when we prayed "The Sinner's Prayer" and invited Jesus to dwell in our hearts.

In Revelation 3:19-22 Jesus says, "Those whom I love I rebuke and discipline. So be earnest, and repent. Here I am! I stand at the door and knock. If anyone hears my voice and opens the door, I will come in and eat with him, and he with me. To him who overcomes, I will give the right to sit with me on my throne, just as I overcame and sat down with my Father on his throne. He who has an ear, let him hear what the Spirit says to the churches."

In general conversations, statements are often made about how so and so "saved" someone, but the truth of this is that our Heavenly Father uses other people to teach us about the salvation experience. Then the Holy Spirit leads us to acceptance of Jesus Christ as our Lord and Savior.

As a speaker for Christian Women's Clubs, I have led thousands of ladies in praying "The Sinner's Prayer," but I take no credit for the personal salvation of any of these ladies, though many signed commitment cards, or expressed to me that they used that opportunity to invite Jesus into their hearts.

Reverend Billy Graham has led millions of people in the sinner's prayer, and hundreds of thousands (perhaps millions) have walked forward to publicly pray, and ask for forgiveness as they invite Jesus into their hearts. Our Father God has used this man in more ways than I can write about and he, himself, wonders why God picked him, "a simple farm boy," to reach all the people he has reached.

Baptist churches do believe in altar calls, just as Dr. Graham does. We feel that a public acknowledgement of our prayer for forgiveness of our sins, and the desire to be a part of the church, the Body of Christ, is part of our salvation experience. There are scriptures in God's Holy Word that apply to this and to our belief in baptism by full immersion. These are as follows:

Romans 3:23: "...for all have sinned and fall short of the glory of God..."

Romans 5:8: "But God demonstrates His own love for us in this: While we were still sinners, Christ died for us."

Romans 10:9: "That if you confess with your mouth, 'Jesus is Lord,' and believe in your heart that God raised Him from the dead, you will be saved."

Ephesians 2:8-9: "For it is by grace you have been saved, through faith – and this not from yourselves, it is the gift of God – not by works, so that no one can boast."

If you do not have a personal relationship with our Lord and Savior, Jesus Christ, an example of "The Sinner's Prayer" is as follows:

"Our Father, I know I am a sinner. I believe Jesus died to forgive me of my sins. I now accept your offer of eternal life. Thank you for forgiving me of all my sin. Thank you for my new life. From this day forward, I will choose to follow you. Amen."

IN THE TWINKLING OF AN EYE

In the New Testament, First Corinthians 15 is called "the Resurrection Chapter." Verses 1-11 describes the "Resurrection of Christ." In verses 12-34, Paul teaches about the "Resurrection of the Dead." Verses 35-58 teach us about "the Resurrection Body." Though the word "rapture" is not used in verses 50-58, many Christians consider this as a description of "The Rapture."

Verse 51 in the NIV Bible reads, "Listen I tell you a mystery; we will not all sleep, but we will all be changed in a flash, in the twinkling of an eye, at the last trumpet."

The verses in Second Corinthians 5:6-10 are frequently summed up with this phrase, "Absence from the body is presence with the Lord." This article didn't start out as a Bible study, but God led me to these scriptures after the thought, "in the twinkling of an eye," entered my mind one morning at the Wound Care Center.

These scriptures help us to understand how fast our soul will be in the presence of our Lord and Savior, the Most High God, our Counselor, and the Prince of Peace, when our physical body dies.

That will be the fastest trip a Christian has ever taken. Throughout our earthly lives, most of us have taken short trips, long vacations, and rides on bumpy country roads. Many folks travel daily on the smooth interstates right into their future.

Sometimes we've been stopped by "traffic jams" created by our own carelessness and/or the actions of others. These are not always on the highways or byways, but sometimes in our own minds.

Health problems, financial woes, and other warring factors have often taken us on some of those huge old-fashioned wooden roller coaster rides. (I can't compare this to the new-fangled upside down coasters as I would never be brave enough to climb aboard one of those.)

Many of us have scaled high mountains only to find ourselves tumbling down into the valley or crevices of anxiety or despair. These bouts often happened "in the twinkling of an eye." At times, things changed so fast that we were not even sure what happened.

A lot of readers have traveled with me through some stormy times when I wondered if the Lord was sending another flood, but then I was reminded of God's promise to Noah in Genesis 9: 1-17. Those rains ended and the sun shone once again, just as one season always follows another, and as the "good" follows the "bad," and vice versa.

A few months ago, I had climbed to the top of the mountain once again. I was starting to walk with the rolling walker (even in and out of a few restaurants), was taking physical therapy, swimming laps, and even losing weight again (14 pounds, ladies!). I thought I was finally going to be "the rolling stone that would gather no more moss."

And then Sunday morning, November 4, 2007, "in the twinkling of an eye," I accidentally caught my sleeve on a cup of boiling grits, and it spilled between my body and my power wheelchair. The pain was immediate, and I struggled to stand so I could remove my pajamas which were adhering to my skin.

I transferred from the chair to the bed and proceeded to make the necessary calls. My daughter happened to have some appropriate burn cream and came to clean up the mess. After the paramedics arrived and talked by phone with the doctor, it was mutually decided that I would wait until Monday to go to the doctor.

I've been treated at the Wound Care Center twice a week and three times in the emergency room when the bandages would not stay fastened. According to the encouraging nurses in the center, the burn is healing correctly; but after six weeks, I've experienced a few major pity parties. Then I remind myself that if I had boiled four cups of water instead of only one, I would probably still be confined to a burn center somewhere with everything from my waist down involved, instead of just one hip and leg. (This was one of those rare occasions when I did not have "The Tray" I once wrote about in my lap...lesson learned.)

While this was happening to me, in other places sick people were dying from illnesses, accidents, and all kinds of violence. Those who were Christians were already in the arms of the Lord long before the paramedics arrived at my house (and they arrived fast).

Isn't it encouraging when we understand that, in spite of our failures, sins, or mistakes, we can look forward to the second resurrection of our Lord. Over 2,000 years ago, He came as a baby, grew in wisdom and stature as Emmanuel (God with us), was crucified and resurrected after three days, and because He is our savior, we can look forward to meeting him "in the twinkling of an eye."

Joy to the world!

WHAT LEGACY WILL I LEAVE IN THIS WORLD?

Another Sunday morning of listening to Dr. Charles Stanley left me deep in thought. His sermon was "What legacy will I leave in this world?" He talked about our purpose here on this earth. He discussed what people today consider a legacy to be. I researched the word "legacy" in my very old dictionary, and this is how it reads:

1. Money or property bequeathed to someone by a will

2. Something handed down from an ancestor.

Well, I certainly will not be leaving a legacy that includes any great financial contribution. With the cost of living constantly going up, I may outlive my income. I pray that for my daughters I will leave a legacy of love, the memories of the loving relationship between their father and me, and our love for them.

For my grandchildren: My travel journals perhaps will teach them about some of our many adventures. I hope to leave stories about their Papa Joe, and how much he would have loved them. Through the stories, I pray they will remember those few years when I was physically able to do more fun things with them.

I pray that through my writings, I have left a legacy of my love for the Lord. I hope that I have been a blessing and an inspiration to others who have suffered from various illnesses.

My desire, through my service to the Lord as a Christian speaker, is that the Holy Spirit has, and will, lead people to personal relationships with Jesus Christ. To be known as a "soul winner" for the Lord is the greatest legacy that I can leave.

It is my prayer that I will leave an example of "fruits" that were important to me: love, joy, peace, patience, kindness, goodness, faithfulness, gentleness, self-control, forgiveness, generosity, cleanliness, thankfulness, willingness to serve, and an ear to listen.

I believe I've been known as a good listener, and perhaps will be remembered by some as a good friend who willingly made time for them. I pray that anyone I had a difference of opinion with will forgive me in the same manner that I forgave them. Many times my world was turned upside down and forgiveness was so very important in my life. I pray that the importance of forgiveness is part of the legacy I will leave when the Lord calls me home.

Honesty is another part of the legacy I hope to leave. Sometimes I may have been too honest, as in the quote "if the shoe fits, wear it." Though I may not have been the most tactful person, I believe I have been known as an honest one. There were times when my honesty may have caused some hurt feelings, but again, this is where I hope I've been forgiven.

What legacy will you leave in this world? Take time to think about this, search your heart, and pray that the Lord will guide you in being a Christian example to your family and friends. That's the legacy I want to leave.